New Hope For Youth

EXPERIENTIAL EXERCISES FOR CHILDREN & ADOLESCENTS

by Robert E. Longo
with
Deborah P. Longo

NEARI Press

New Hope for Youth: Experiential Exercises for Children and Adolescents

Published by
NEARI Press
70 North Summer Street
Holyoke, MA 01040
413.540.0712

Distributed by
Whitman Distribution
10 Water Street
PO Box 1220
Lebanon, New Hampshire 03766
603.448.0037
800.353.3730

ISBN# 1-929657-20-X

Price US $35.00

ACKNOWLEDGMENTS

This book was written as a guide for clinicians and professional staff working with youth at the various facilities th. make up the New Hope Treatment Centers (NHTC). Over the years New Hope has strived to bring training to its sta that addresses the many models and treatments used with children and adolescents who are admitted to our res dential facilities. NHTC has tried to stay current with emerging treatments, models and philosophies regarding clinic. work with troubled youth. Part of this effort is to bring the best trainers we can find to NHTC to train our staff, and t have staff attend national conferences. A good part of our program development has been to look at moving beyon using just traditional therapies, treatments, and models and learning to think outside of the box. The result has bee to increase the amount of experiential work we do with our patients.

The combined experience of the authors in working with youth extends more than 50 years. We have conducted hur dreds of training events independently and together, and have also attended numerous conferences and trainin events since 1975. We have participated in numerous exercises at conferences and training events and/or hear speakers discuss them and their use with a variety of patients.

Some of these exercises have been handed down from one trainer to the next without acknowledgment or recognitio of the original developer or publication from which they were learned. Therefore, it is hard to determine who has actu ally developed some of the exercises in this book. All exercises that are not original have the source noted at the en of that exercise. Many of the exercises contained in this book, if not original, have been modified in order to be currer and useful with a youthful population. We apologize now for any oversight on our part. While reading this book, if yo by chance recognize a particular exercise and its source/origin, we would greatly appreciate hearing from you so tha we can give the proper person(s) and/or publication their well-deserved credit.

Our heartfelt thanks goes to Diane Langelier and Lisa Harris for reviewing and editing portions of this book. While work ing at NHTC, Lisa took the time to read over the initial draft. We also want to acknowledge the many therapists an patients at NHTC for working with us, allowing us to do exercises in group therapy sessions and training sessions, an taking the time to explore using these exercises in group therapy sessions. In addition we would like to thank Cind Tyo and Matt Doyle, both from New Hope Treatment Centers for contributing exercises to this book.

We attempted to contact Sue Forbess-Greene as we have cited several exercises in a book authored by her (se References). Our attempts to contact her and the publisher did not work, but we want to acknowledge Sue, Su Robinson, Jim Haaven, Charlene Steen, Mark Bartleson, Pat Van Buren and L. Lowenstein for exercises as well.

We would also like to acknowledge and thank John Bergman of the Geese Theatre Company in East Swanzey, Ne Hampshire for reviewing the final draft of this book and contributing many of the exercises within. John is a friend, co league, and has served as a mentor to us in doing experiential work, especially in the areas of role-plays and dram therapy. As a master drama therapist his guidance, suggestions, and feedback have been invaluable. Thank you Johr

CONTENTS

NTRODUCTION AND OVERVIEW: HOW TO USE THIS BOOK

Ve have spent the majority of our respective careers working with people and predominantly working with children and adolescents. Our combined experience covers a vast area of work in both community-based and residential settings, vith normal functioning patients1, those with learning disabilities, and lower-functioning patients, both male and emale, and youth with a wide variety of problems in varied life circumstances.

Ve have worked with youth who have been abused sexually, physically, emotionally, and psychologically, as well as hildren who have been victims of neglect and/or suffer from attachment disorders. We have worked with youth who ave engaged in violent acts including the sexual abuse of others, and with youth who have run away from home nd/or have been labeled as incorrigible.

n our work, most of our patients have been youth who have suffered loss, death of family members, placements in oster care and/or in adoptive homes, and youth who have had problems but remained in an intact family that has been villing to work toward their child's improved health and recovery. During the past few years we have focused most of ur work with children and adolescents in residential treatment settings. For purposes of this book, and based upon ur current experience, we will refer to children, adolescents, males, and females as patients.

Ve have tried to organize this book in several different ways. The exercises are organized by ease of use, potential lifficulty, and level of intrusiveness. The exercises are divided into chapters titled Warm-up Exercises **(W)**, Introductory Exercises **(I)**, Intermediate Exercises **(M)**, and Advanced Exercises **(A)**. Each exercise is level indicated with **W**, **I**, **A**, or **A** before the number of the exercise, and titled, e.g., the first exercise in this book is titled/labeled Exercise **W 1 · MONSTER LEGS**. The title Exercise **W** indicates it is a warm-up level exercise, "1" indicates it is exercise num- er one in this category, and "Monster Legs" is the name of the exercise. Some exercises are double labeled with two evels as they appear to fall in between two levels.

Vhen using experiential treatments it is always necessary to warm-up groups that are new and where members are ot familiar with each other. Even groups that have worked together for a period of time can benefit from warm-up exer- ises to set the mood for more advanced work. One does not want to jump into advanced work without first working he group through easier and less-threatening exercises. When using experiential exercises, you will find that most atients engaged in this work learn gradually. Patients learning and becoming more comfortable with this work occurs s they work through the various types and levels of exercises. The exercises often build upon each other, and there- ore, patients learn in stages.

After each exercise we have placed a summary table (see Figure 1). The summary table is useful to give the facilita- or a quick reference and overview of the exercise, and includes eight categories for each exercise.

First, we identify the purpose of each exercise, which we discuss at the beginning of the exercise. If the exercise's bjective is to develop group cohesion and trust, we note that under the purpose section. In some cases the exercis- s serve multiple purposes which are noted, i.e., exercises that promote trust, team work, involve movement to ener- jize the participants, and touch, etc.

Second, each chart indicates the level of that particular exercise: Warm-up Exercises **(W)**, Introductory Exercises **(I)**, ntermediate Exercises **(M)**, and Advanced Exercises **(A)**.

Third, we have identified exercises by participation style, based upon the use of groups. Some exercises can be or hould be done with a large group **(LG)**; most warm-up exercises should be done with the entire group regardless of he group's size. Other exercises require that the participants be divided into smaller groups of a certain size in order o conduct the exercise properly **(SG)**. Some exercises require participants to work in pairs **(P)** such as in role-plays, r can be done on an individual basis in one-to-one counseling/therapy sessions **(IC)**.

Normal functioning refers to patients of average or better I.Q. and with few or no learning disabilities.

Fourth, we have estimated the appropriate amount of time (in minutes) necessary to conduct each exercise using standard group of 10-12 people. If the group you are working with has 20 people, then the time would be increase and possibly doubled; with 30 people the time possibly could be tripled and so forth, unless otherwise indicated. Alway allow a little extra time to conduct the exercise, and then time to process the exercise with the group.

Fifth, we have indicated whether the exercise requires certain materials such as music, art supplies, handouts, fli chart paper, rolls of newsprint, crayons, pens, paint, old magazines, etc. You should review the exercise first befor conducting it to make sure necessary supplies are readily available. Exercises involving music will have recommend ed songs or types of music to be used. One can be creative and select music of one's choosing in most cases. If ther are worksheets for the exercise they can be found in Appendix A. If the exercise requires a lot of movement we sug gest that the room be cleared of furniture and pointed or sharp objects to avoid accidental injury.

Sixth, we have attempted to indicate any cautions/precautions necessary and associated with the exercise. Som exercises require a lot of physical activity. We use a physical activity level **(PAL)** to indicate the level of activity: low **(L)** medium **(M)**, and high **(H)**. Low means there is minimal and in some cases no physical exertion on the part of partici pants and high indicates there is a lot of physical exertion that might parallel exercising. Medium is the level betwee low and high and means that there will be some physical exertion but not excessive and not low. Patients or person with physical limitations or disabilities should be given a warning about the exercise and the option to not participate

Seventh, if the exercise can be modified, you will find a **YES** in this category, which indicates we have included one o more possible variations for that particular exercise.

Eighth, we have developed a set of process questions for many of the exercises. **YES** in this category means we hav listed one or more suggested process questions for that particular exercise. Process questions are suggested ques tions only and they can be modified or eliminated at the discretion of the group facilitator (the clinician or trainer con ducting the exercise). All exercises should be debriefed/processed immediately afterward with the participants. A se of basic process questions is on page 34.

FIGURE-1 SAMPLE EXERCISE SUMMARY TABLE

Purpose	Description
Level	**W, I, M, or A**
Group size	**LG, SG, P,** and/or **IC**
Time ~ in minutes	Estimated number of minutes to complete exercise
Materials needed	As indicated
Cautions	None; or as indicated, **PAL = L, M, or H**
Variations	None or **YES**
Process questions	Basic or **YES**

Although this book is designed primarily for use with children and adolescents, we encourage anyone using these exercises to first experience the exercise before doing it with a patient or group of patients. One way of understanding the exercises and ensuring their success is to practice them by yourself or with other colleagues or friends. Therefore, these exercises can also serve the function of staff training and development.

Become familiar with them and the potential outcomes. When conducting the exercise with patients, the facilitator and all persons present should participate in them. You need to be sensitive to your level of comfort with these activities. Many people are reluctant to participate in experiential exercises because they are shy, uncomfortable, and/or embarrassed doing activities in front of others. If you are not willing to participate in them, it may be best that you not facilitate them.

We hope you find the exercises contained herein useful in your work. They can be fun for everyone involved while promoting personal growth and healing. As we noted above, if you know the source of an exercise that is not referenced we would like to hear from you. We are also interested in hearing from you if you know variations of exercises, related exercises, or new and different exercises. Good luck in your work!

Robert E. Longo
New Hope Treatment Centers
Summerville, S.C.

Deborah Price Longo
Charleston, S.C.

CHAPTER ONE

LEARNING STYLES, CHILD DEVELOPMENT, AND EXPERIENTIAL TREATMENTS

LEARNING STYLES

The use of experiential therapies with youth is an effective treatment method that enhances standard cognitive-behavioral treatment. The use of experiential exercises can facilitate treatment, add new and different insight to patient learning, and enrich the overall treatment experience. This is especially true when one takes into account that individuals have different learning styles.

The ancient Chinese proverb, *"Tell me I forget; Show me I remember; Involve me I understand",* summarizes the value of experiential work. Not all people respond well to traditional sit-down, verbal/linguistic learning styles. Integrated (holistic) treatment seeks to bring a variety of theories and models into the treatment process to enhance a person's potential. For example, Howard Gardner (1983), a Harvard researcher noted for his work on multiple intelligences, teaches us that children have a variety of learning styles and abilities and suggests there are seven learning styles common to children. These learning styles include Verbal/Linguistic Intelligence, Visual/Spatial Intelligence, Musical/Rhythmic Intelligence, Body/Kinesthetic Intelligence, Logical/Mathematical Intelligence, Interpersonal Intelligence, and Intrapersonal Intelligence. He notes that of the seven multiple intelligences, most people are taught using Verbal/Linguistic teaching styles. The use of experiential therapies opens avenues for patients to use all seven multiple intelligences and thus have a better opportunity to learn and grow while in treatment. The multiple intelligences are described briefly below with examples.

Verbal/Linguistic Intelligence. Verbal/Linguistic Intelligence is related to the use of words and language, both written and spoken. The use of and reliance upon this intelligence dominates most western educational systems and includes poetry, humor, story-telling, use of metaphors, grammar, symbolic thinking, abstract reasoning, and conceptual patterning, reading and writing.

This is the intelligence most treatment programs for youth rely upon, as they incorporate a variety of reading and writing assignments. Use of this intelligence is also used in sit down individual and group therapies and psycho-educational classes. For children who do not learn well with this intelligence, it is possible that the patient will not do well in treatment, may drop out of treatment, or fail in treatment. Examples of methods to develop this intelligence include:

Vocabulary development
Reading
Formal speech
Creative writing
Humor/jokes

Experiential exercises that enhance this learning style include:

Journal/Diary keeping
Verbal debate
Impromptu speaking
Storytelling

Visual/Spatial Intelligence. Visual/Spatial Intelligence deals with such things as the visual arts (including painting, drawing, and sculpture); navigation, map-making and architecture (which involve the use of space and knowing how to get around in it); and games which require the ability to visualize objects from different perspectives and angles such as chess. The key sensory base of Visual/Spatial Intelligence is the sense of sight, and being able to form mental images/pictures in the mind and to visualize objects.

For children who do not work well with the verbal/linguistic style of learning, this intelligence can be a primary mode of learning and assimilating information. Experiential therapies are useful in working with those who use this form of intelligence. Examples of methods to develop this intelligence include:

Color schemes
Patterns/designs
Pictures

Experiential exercises that enhance this learning style include:

Guided imagery
Art therapy
Painting
Drawing
Sculpture

Musical/Rhythmic Intelligence. Musical/Rhythmic Intelligence includes such capacities as the recognition and use of rhythmic and tonal patterns, including sensitivity to various environmental sounds, the human voice, and musical instruments. Many of us learned the alphabet through this intelligence by singing the "A-B-C song". Of all forms of intelligence, the consciousness altering effect of music and rhythm on the brain is probably the greatest. Examples of methods to develop this intelligence include:

Rhythmic patterns
Vocal sounds/tones
Percussion vibration
Humming
Environmental sounds
Instrumental sounds
Singing
Tonal patterns
Music performance
Music composition

Experiential exercises that enhance this learning style include:

Combining art therapy with music
Using music in conjunction with various experiential exercises

Body/Kinesthetic Intelligence. Body/Kinesthetic Intelligence is related to physical movement and the knowing/wisdom of the body, including the brain's motor cortex, which controls bodily motion. This intelligence relies on the ability to use the body to express emotions (as in dance and body language), to play a game, and to create a new product. It is "learning by doing" which has long been recognized as an important part of education. Our bodies know things our minds do not know and cannot learn in any other way. For example, our bodies know how to ride a bike, roller skate, and type. Examples of methods to develop this intelligence include:

Folk/creative dance
Physical exercise
Inventing
Martial arts

Experiential exercises that enhance this learning style include:

Exercises involving movement
Role-playing
Physical gesturing
Drama therapy
Mime

Logical/Mathematical Intelligence. Logical/Mathematical Intelligence is most often associated with scientific thinking and inductive reasoning. This intelligence involves the capacity to recognize patterns, work with abstract symbols (such as numbers and geometric shapes), and discern relationships and/or connections between separate and distinct pieces of information. Patients who suffer with developmental delays and learning disabilities may not rely upon this form of intelligence for learning. Examples of methods to develop this intelligence include:

Outlining
Calculation
Number sequences
Deciphering codes

Experiential exercises that enhance this learning style include:

Problem solving
Pattern games

Interpersonal Intelligence. Interpersonal Intelligence involves the ability to work cooperatively with others in a group as well as the ability to communicate, verbally and nonverbally, with other people. This intelligence builds on the capacity to notice distinctions among others; for example, contrasts in moods, temperament, motivations, and intentions. Thus, interpersonal intelligence operates primarily through person-to-person relationships and communication. In the more advanced forms of this intelligence, one can literally pass over into another's perspective and read their intentions and desires. One can have a genuine empathy for another's feelings, fears, anticipations, and beliefs.

When this intelligence is used, the therapeutic relationship can be extremely powerful in teaching patients and supporting them through the treatment process. Examples of methods to develop this intelligence include:

Intuiting others' feelings
Person-to-person communication
Cooperative learning strategies
Sensing others' motives

Experiential exercises that enhance this learning style include:

Empathy practices
Collaboration skills
Giving feedback
Receiving feedback
Group projects

Intrapersonal Intelligence. Intrapersonal Intelligence involves knowledge of the internal aspects of the self, such as knowledge of feelings, the range of emotional responses, thinking processes, self-reflection, and a sense of intuition about spiritual realities. Intrapersonal intelligence allows us to be conscious of our consciousness: that is, to step back from ourselves and watch ourselves as an outside observer. It involves our capacity to experience wholeness and unity, to discern patterns of connection with the larger order of things, and connection with people, to perceive higher states of consciousness, to experience the lure of the future, and to dream of and actualize the possible.

In working with youth with behavioral problems it is not likely that this intelligence has been developed and one facet of treatment will be to develop this intelligence in order to promote the patient's ability to develop relationships, empathy, and work with unhealthy thinking patterns. If this intelligence is not developed as a part of treatment, there is less likelihood that cognitive restructuring and emotional development will realize its fullest potential as part of the treatment process. Most certainly, the lack of developing this intelligence will effect attachment and the ability to form meaningful relationships. Examples of methods to develop this intelligence include:

Silent meditation/reflection
Focusing/concentration skills

Experiential exercises that enhance this learning style include:

Mindfulness practices
Centering practices
Thinking strategies
Emotional processing
Complex guided imagery

CHILD DEVELOPMENT

Whether you work with children who are average, above average, or children who are developmentally delayed or have learning disabilities, it is important to adjust exercises and focus on learning styles that are suited to the patient's level of understanding or ability. Age and the patient's stage of developmental are important to factor into doing this work. Understanding the work of Piaget, Erikson, and Kohlberg[2] can serve as a guide to understanding a patient's developmental abilities and learning styles.

PRESCHOOL-AGE CHILDREN

Physical Characteristics of the Preschool-Age Child

Preschool children (age 3-5) are very active, and enjoy running, climbing, and jumping. Frequent rest periods are required, as much energy is spent in these activities. Children at this age need to be supervised and directed in their activities so that the teacher/parent/caregiver does not lose control. Large muscles are more developed than the child's small-motor control. Large items/toys i.e., building blocks, crayons, etc. should be used so the child will be able to handle them easily. Eye-hand coordination may be less than perfect. Large print books are easier for them to read. The skull bones are still soft, and therefore, special attention is paid to activities in order to avoid possible head injuries.

Social Characteristics of the Preschool-Age Child

Preschoolers are very flexible socially. Friendships are usually within their own gender, but friends of the opposite sex are not uncommon, and playgroups will change rapidly. Quarrels are frequent, but usually resolved quickly. Different types of play are demonstrated based on social class, gender, and circumstances affecting free play (availability of toys, place to play, etc.).

Emotional Characteristics of the Preschool-Age Child

Children of this age are very emotional. Children share their emotions frequently. Jealousy is inevitable, as each child is competing for the parent's/caregiver's/teacher's attention.

---

[2] http://tip.psychology.org/piaget.html
http://www.nd.edu/~rbarger/kohlberg.html
http://psychology.about.com/library/weekly/aa091500a.htm

Cognitive Characteristics of the Preschool-Age Child

Preschoolers will stick to their own rules in language development, rather than accept corrections given by others. Interaction, interest, opportunities, urging, limits, admiration, and displays of affection encourage competence. Authoritative parents are most successful in fostering competent children. These parents set boundaries, but are loving and compassionate.

TABLE 1

COMPARISON OF ERICKSON'S, PIAGET'S, AND KOHLBERG'S VIEWS ON PRESCHOOL CHILDREN 3-5

Erikson's Views: Preschool-Age Child

Autonomy versus Shame and Doubt. Toddlers that are able to find some independence in doing what they are capable of doing and are properly supervised, form a sense of autonomy. If these explorations are suppressed however, by the parents or teachers, the child may begin to doubt their abilities or feel ashamed of their actions.

Initiative versus Guilt. An elaborate form of autonomy, initiative is the addition of planning and undertaking a task, rather than just exploring places and ideas. Exploration and experimentation should be encouraged by the teachers and parents. Guilty feelings occur when the child's activities are considered pointless or boring by the parent or teacher, or if the adult is annoyed by these actions.

Piaget's Views: Preschool-Age Child

Preoperational Stage: Gradually acquires ability to conserve and decenter but not capable of operational thinking and unable to mentally reverse actions.

Kohlberg's Views: Preschool-Age Child

Pre-moral

Stage 1: Punishment-Obedience Orientation: Physical consequences determine good and bad behavior. The authority has superior power and determines good and bad. Punishment is avoided by staying out of trouble.

Stage 2: Instrumental-Relativist Orientation: Actions are right when they are instrumental in satisfying one's own needs or involves an even exchange. Obeying rules should bring benefits in return.

PRIMARY-AGE CHILDREN

Physical Characteristics of the Primary-Age Child

The high energy of primary-age children (age 6-8), combined with the frequent classroom situations used by teachers, encourages children to form nervous habits, such as chewing on pens and pencils, fingernail biting, and fidgeting. Rest periods are still needed to balance the energetic play periods, and naps may still be required for some children. Fine-motor skills are still lacking, especially in boys. Focusing on small print may be difficult and may lead to eye fatigue. Children may put themselves into danger because of extreme physical activity. Reckless play should be discouraged because of the risk of injury, especially since bones are not yet fully developed.

Social Characteristics of the Primary-Age Child

Children of this age tend to be more selective in their friends and they usually have a best friend. Organized games are popular, but there may be controversy in setting rules or team spirit. Quarrels are still common, although they tend to be more verbal than physical. Boys in particular are prone to engage in punching and wrestling.

Emotional Characteristics of the Primary-Age Child

Children of this age are eager to please parents/caregivers/teachers. Primary-age children are sensitive to criticism and find it hard to handle failure. Frequent praise and recognition should be used by parents, caregivers, and those working with children. Children become increasingly sensitive to others' feelings as empathy develops, however, personal attacks to hurt others are common and without the child realizing the deep emotional impact on the other child.

Cognitive Characteristics of the Primary-Age Child

Primary grade children are eager to learn, and therefore, self-motivation is high. These children like to talk and their language skills are demonstrated better in their speech than in their writing. Literal interpretation of rules may inspire students to become tattletales. Therefore, acknowledge the child for reporting the wrong doing, but don't praise the child for telling on his/her classmates.

TABLE 2

COMPARISON OF ERICKSON'S, PIAGET'S, AND KOHLBERG'S VIEWS ON PRIMARY AGE CHILDREN 6-8

ERIKSON S VIEWS: PRIMARY-AGE CHILD	PIAGET S VIEWS: PRIMARY-AGE CHILD	KOHLBERG S VIEWS PRIMARY-AGE CHILD
Industry versus Inferiority: Intellectual curiosity prompts students of this age to be creative and industrious. Teachers and parents should encourage this creativity, as this stage is a key stage in a student's academic development. Inferiority occurs when the child is discouraged and has the feeling that their academic work is worthless. School work seems tedious and boring. These children have the belief that they will not excel in their schoolwork.	Preoperational Stage: Gradually acquires ability to conserve and decenter but not capable of operational thinking and unable to mentally reverse actions. Concrete Operational Stage: Capable of operations, but solves problems by generalizing from concrete experiences. Manipulation of conditions is difficult unless the child has experienced such conditions.	Stage 1: Punishment-Obedience Orientation: Physical consequences determine good and bad behavior. The authority has superior power and determines good and bad. Punishment is avoided by staying out of trouble. Stage 2: Instrumental-Relativist Orientation: Actions are right when they are instrumental in satisfying one's own needs or involves an even exchange. Obeying rules should bring benefits in return.

ELEMENTARY-AGE CHILDREN

Physical Characteristics of the Elementary-Age Child

Elementary-age boys and girls (ages 9-10) are leaner and stronger. Girls may be slightly taller and heavier than boys. Gender confusion may result due to similarity in hairstyles and clothing. Obesity is an issue with some children, as junk food and lack of physical activity may contribute to problems with body weight/height ratios. Gender differences display themselves in athletic abilities. Boys tend to be more skilled in baseball and basketball, whereas girls are usually more skilled in gymnastics. Growth is usually predictable, although there may be some 'early bloomers' that will begin puberty during this time.

Social Characteristics of the Elementary-Age Child

The peer group is much more central in the elementary-age child's life, and it is the child's peers that determine social standards. Friendships are more selective and gender-based. This is the age when Boy Scouts, Girl Scouts, team sports, and other similar activities are popular. Avoidance of the opposite sex when possible is commonly seen.

Emotional Characteristics of the Elementary-Age Child

Self-image is developed during this stage. Self-concept entails physical, social, cognitive, and emotional characteristics, while self-esteem entails judgments that children make about their personal characteristics. Disruptive family relationships, social rejection, and school failure may lead to delinquent behavior. Delinquents often have few friends, short attention spans, and do poorly in school due to a lack of basic skills.

Cognitive Characteristics of the Elementary-Age Child

Logical thinking is constrained and inconsistent. Differences in cognitive style are apparent. The tendencies to respond to different intellectual tasks in different ways are shown by these children. Some students prefer structure, whereas some students would rather work on their own initiative. Impulsive students tend to give quick responses to questions while reflective students think things through before they answer.

TABLE 3

COMPARISON OF ERICKSON'S, PIAGET'S, AND KOHLBERG'S VIEWS ON ELEMENTARY AGE CHILDREN 9-10

Erikson's Views: Elementary-Age Child

Industry versus Inferiority: Intellectual curiosity prompts students of this age to be creative and industrious. Teachers and parents should encourage this creativity, as this stage is a key stage in a student's academic development. Inferiority occurs when the child is discouraged and has the feeling that their academic work is worthless. School work seems tedious and boring. These children have the belief that they will not excel in their schoolwork.

Piaget's Views: Elementary-Age Child

Concrete Operational Stage: Capable of operations, but solves problems by generalizing from concrete experiences. Manipulation of conditions is difficult unless the child has experienced such conditions.

Kohlberg's Views: Elementary-Age Child

Stage 1: Punishment-Obedience Orientation: Physical consequences determine good and bad behavior. The authority has superior power and determines good and bad. Punishment is avoided by staying out of trouble.

Stage 2: Instrumental-Relativist Orientation: Actions are right when they are instrumental in satisfying one's own needs or involves an even exchange. Obeying rules should bring benefits in return.

Stage 3: Good Boy-Nice Girl Orientation: The right actions will impress other people.

Stage 4: Law-and-Order Orientation: In order to maintain social order, rules must be established and followed. Respecting authority is critical in maintaining order.

MIDDLE SCHOOL-AGE CHILDREN

Physical Characteristics of the Middle School-Age Child

Children of the middle school-age (age 11-13) go through puberty at different rates and times. Growth spurts can be rapid and uneven. Early-maturing girls are sometimes embarrassed about their growth spurts and tend to be less confident and popular. Early-maturing boys are often very confident, high in self-esteem, and are leaders among their peers. Late-maturing girls are outgoing and tend to be more accepted by their peers. Late-maturing boys sometimes demand attention through immature behavior and they tend to feel inferior. Curiosity about sex increases in this age group, and parents and educators should address human sexuality education and health focused courses.

Social Characteristics of the Middle School-Age Child

Interpersonal reasoning, or the ability to understand relationships between motives and behaviors in groups of people, is developed in this stage. Conformity is highest among middle school students, which explains the popularity of certain items such as shoes, clothes, jewelry, or backpacks.

Emotional Characteristics of the Middle School-Age Child

This is the "Storm and Stress" period for many pre-adolescents and early adolescents. Feelings of confusion, anxiety, and depression are evident in this age group. Many children are self-conscious and self-centered, and feel that adults just don't understand what they are going through in adolescence.

Cognitive Characteristics of the Middle School-Age Child

Self-efficacy, the concept that one feels capable of doing certain things is apparent among middle school children. Gender differences are decreasing among this age group, although some studies show that girls feel inferior in certain subjects and, therefore, achieve less in these areas.

TABLE 4

COMPARISON OF ERICKSON'S, PIAGET'S, AND KOHLBERG'S VIEWS ON MIDDLE SCHOOL CHILDREN 11-13

Erikson's Views: Middle School-Age Child

Identity versus Role Confusion: The development of one's identity is critical at this stage, as children progress through adolescence and become an adult. Role confusion occurs when children are unsure about what behaviors will be reacted to favorably. Some children develop negative identity characteristics, which demonstrate themselves in the form of rebellion and attempts to display individuality.

Piaget's Views: Middle School-Age Child

Formal Operational Stage: Ability to deal with abstractions, form hypotheses, solve problems systematically, engage in mental manipulations. Logical processes are developed in this stage.

Kohlberg's Views: Middle School-Age Child

Conventional

Stage 3: Good Boy-Nice Girl Orientation: The right actions will impress other people.

Stage 4: Law-and-Order Orientation: In order to maintain social order, rules must be established and followed. Respecting authority is critical in maintaining order.

HIGH SCHOOL-AGE CHILDREN

Physical Characteristics of the High School-Age Child

Most high school-age children (age 14-18) have reached puberty, and have matured fully. However, some boys do continue to grow even after high school. Many students engage in sexual activity, but they usually do not form sexual relationships well. Sexual activity may lead to unwanted pregnancy or sexually transmitted diseases.

Social Characteristics of the High School-Age Child

Parents tend to influence long-range plans, while peers influence short-term planning and spontaneous events. Girls experience greater anxiety about friendships than boys. After-school employment is common among high-school students, as it helps students develop responsibility and gives them independence and self-confidence. However, having a job reduces available time for studying, extra-curricular activities, socialization, and sleep.

Emotional Characteristics of the High School-Age Child

Psychiatric disorders manifest themselves during high school. Eating disorders, substance abuse, schizophrenia, depression, and suicidal tendencies are demonstrated in this age group. Encouraging success in learning will help students that suffer from depression, which when severe, may lead to suicide.

Cognitive Characteristics of the High School-Age Child

Formal thought can be executed by most students, although some students choose not to. Using prior knowledge to accomplish new tasks will encourage formal thought. Political thinking becomes more abstract, liberal, and knowledgeable.

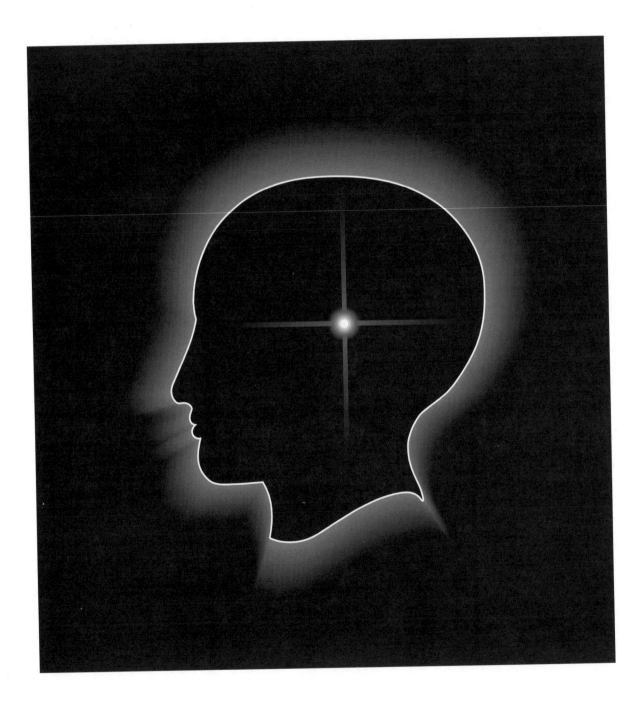

TABLE 5

COMPARISON OF ERICKSON'S, PIAGET'S, AND KOHLBERG'S VIEWS ON HIGH SCHOOL CHILDREN 14-18

Erikson's Views: High School-Age Children

Identity versus Role Confusion: The development of one's identity is critical at this stage, as the child progresses through adolescence and becomes an adult. Role confusion occurs when children are unsure about what behaviors will be reacted to favorably. Some children develop negative identity characteristics, which demonstrate themselves in the form of rebellion and attempts to display individuality.

Intimacy versus Isolation: The development of intimate relationships with other people is the central focus of this stage. Sacrifice and compromise contribute to establishing these relationships. The inability to develop relationships may result in a sense of isolation, or loneliness. This stage may not be reached by all students of high school age, rather, it may occur as late as age 25-30.

Piaget's Views: High School-Age Children

Formal Operational Stage: Ability to deal with abstractions, form hypotheses, solve problems systematically, engage in mental manipulations. Logical processes are developed in this stage.

Kohlberg's Views: High School-Age Children

Stage 3: Good Boy-Nice Girl Orientation: The right actions will impress other people.

Stage 4: Law-and-Order Orientation: In order to maintain social order, rules must be established and followed. Respecting authority is critical in maintaining order.

REACTIVE ATTACHMENT DISORDER[3].

Insecure Attachment and Attachment Disorder (AD) also known as Reactive Attachment Disorder (RAD), which is a relatively new diagnosis to the DSM-IV-TR, is a disorder that is often misunderstood. Insecure attachment (which is not diagnosable) and AD which is, are conditions in which individuals have difficulty forming loving, caring, lasting, intimate, relationships. Attachment and bonding are generally used interchangeably. AD youth usually do not learn how to trust, and often fail to develop a conscience. AD youth learn that the world is not a safe place.

RAD as defined by the American Psychiatric Association's *Diagnostic and Statistical Manual of Mental Disorders Fourth Edition (DSM-IV-TR)*, requires etiological factors, such as gross deprivation of care or successive multiple care givers, for diagnosis. Attachment disordered youth may present in two ways.

In inhibited RAD, the child does not initiate or respond to social interactions in a developmentally appropriate manner. When caregivers are not reliable, consistent, or respond in an unpredictable and uncertain way, the child may not be able to establish a pattern of confident expectation. One result is insecure attachment, a less than optimal internal sense of confidence and trust in others. The child uses psychological defenses to avoid disappointments, which may contribute to a negative working model of relationships that leads to insecurity.

In disinhibited RAD, the child has diffuse attachments, indiscriminate sociability, and excessive familiarity with strangers. These children repeatedly lose attachment figures or have multiple caregivers and have never had the chance to develop a continuous and consistent attachment to at least one caregiver. The usual anxiety and concern with strangers is not present.

AD youth are masters at manipulating their environment and people in their environment. They may demonstrate learning problems in school. Lack of conscious appears to be caused by his or her lack of trust in anyone.

High risk factors for attachment disorders may include:[4]
• maternal ambivalence towards pregnancy
• unprepared mothers with poor parenting skills
• sudden separation from a primary caretaker
• child abuse/neglect
• frequent moves or placements
• traumatic prenatal experience
• inconsistent or inadequate day care

Stimulation from birth on, is especially critical during the first 2-3 years of life. The absence of appropriate stimulation may lead to:[5]
• indiscriminate affection
• extremely demanding or attention seeking behaviors
• autistic like behaviors
• hyperactivity
• aggression (including acts of cruelty)
• temper tantrums
• no cause and effect thinking

---

[3] http://www.emedicine.com/ped/topic2646.htm
[4] Ibid.
[5] Ibid.

Healthy attachment helps facilitate the following [6]:
- the ability to think logically
- the development of a conscious
- the ability to cope with stress and frustration
- becoming self-reliant
- development of relationships
- the ability to handle fear and worry
- the ability to handle any perceived threat to self

Symptoms of Attachment Disorder may include:[7]
- superficially engaging and charming child
- a lack of cause and effect thinking
- indiscriminate affectionate with strangers
- destruction of self, others, and/or things
- developmental lags
- lack of eye contact
- preoccupation with fire, blood, gore
- cruelty to animals and/or siblings
- poor peer relations

- inappropriate demanding or clinging behavior
- stealing or lying
- lack of conscience
- poor impulse control
- fighting for control over everything
- hoarding or gorging food

Successful therapy with these youth will depend upon the therapist's willingness to use unconventional strategies. Some of these strategies are to 1) find and to face the depth of the feelings that these youth keep hidden, 2) revisit the trauma with the child and to communicate that by doing this together; the trauma is not bigger than the child, and the child can overcome it:[8]

Therapists need to be prepared to face the horrors that these youth have experienced if we ever hope to help them heal. Successful therapy needs to be challenging and at times may be intrusive. These interventions are always done while being loving and supportive. Critical goals of treatment may include but are not limited to:
- resolution of early losses
- development of trust
- modulation of affect
- development of internal control
- development of reciprocal relationships
- learning appropriate responses to external structure and societal rules
- correcting distorted thinking patterns
- developing self-respect

EXPERIENTIAL TREATMENT

From a therapeutic standpoint, one criterion for teaching patients effective interventions is using a developmental/contextual perspective that matches treatment to the patient's learning styles, cognitive abilities, developmental stage, and moral development stage. One cannot hope to maximize a patient's potential for personal change if the teaching style treats patients as subjects to be filled with standardized, single track, 'correct' ways of thinking and behaving. In our clinical practice we encourage patients to *become* authentically themselves. We try to avoid having a preset notion of what patients should do therapeutically. Experiential treatments allow patients to learn through self-exploration and self-discovery. This is not to say that we don't teach our patients standard and/or specialized pieces of information through classroom style education. We do. However, we encourage patients, once they have acquired this generalized knowledge, to internalize it in ways that work best for them. We try to give them several healthy and effective choices for therapeutic change, and promote such through frequently using experiential treatments.

[6] Ibid.

[7] Ibid.

[8] Ibid.

Experiential treatments when used properly do not sound like or come across as therapy done *to* patients, but rather *with* them, and often with minimal direction. The challenge in using applied experiential treatments is to learn *with* patients, not just simply teach *at* them. Like with any other therapeutic process, when therapy goes well, both clinician and patient grow and learn.

Behaviors youth employ in particular situations (i.e., acting out when one does not get his/her way) are learned and strengthened through frequent repetition. Over time they become automatic responses to social and other situations. Undesirable, inappropriate learned behavior can be modified through experiential treatments, i.e. role-plays, because these interventions challenge the way youth traditionally think and react to real or perceived situations.

Most behavior is learned, and therefore can be unlearned or relearned. Unlearning requires the patient to focus on the acquisition of new behaviors and then rehearsing them, as one does in most learning situations. New behavior is not learned by simply describing it or telling someone about it. It does not become incorporated into one's life by simple re-enactment and/or one-trial learning. Practice and rehearsal is critical to the learning process. If children practiced social skills in the same manner they practiced sports, dancing, and electronic games, imagine the learning that would take place. Presenting patients with the same information in new and different ways enhances the learning experience.

Verbal therapies (psycho-educational models and group treatment) alone do not often cover everything the patient needs, nor do they include the patient in exploration of what, in his/her eyes, are problem behaviors (versus the beliefs and observations of staff). Experiential treatments and using multiple intelligences can enhance learning and behavioral change.

When patients learn outside of personal experience, it is difficult for the patient to incorporate the acquired knowledge into personal behavior. It is an external rather than internal process. Taught knowledge through verbal/linguistic learning often squelches personal discovery. When youth are taught concrete thinking skills (traditional cognitive therapy) they simply accept information (and often do not use it) rather than explore and discover information by learning to think for themselves.

We believe it is important to challenge the thinking of our patients and help them develop interpersonal and social skills. Learning is enhanced when youth can be the developers of new thinking and behavior rather than just passive participants who learn by traditional and often routine methods. Experiential treatments can be used to help youth look inward for solutions and alternatives, but staff must be careful that the process does not become one of **imitation** rather than original **self-discovery**.

Patients, for example, stereotype themselves through program labeling and by performing behavior through simple routines. In residential programs, patients traditionally learn to restrict themselves to a predictable or limited set of responses based upon program rules, regulations, peer critique, and staff feedback. Over time their thinking, behavior, and responses become automatic and more pronounced. Experiential treatments help us to more effectively see the patient's behavior which is the direct result of their thinking, and which is linked to their various personas both public and private[9]. The private persona however, is one we seldom see in patients. The patient's behavior (the behavior they present when coming into treatment), as in other life situations (how they behaved in their life in the community), is a learned and practiced routine (role) that is adaptive and automatic. If we continue to foster the same type of learning patterns in treatment, patients will learn a new role, the role of being a *patient in treatment*.

James Thompson (1999) notes that the use of experiential treatments, including role-plays, can be undermined by the juvenile justice system where there is inherent limiting of individual role-taking abilities and a negative reinforcement and solidification of certain behaviors. Many of our patients have been subjected to this process, especially if they have been in previous residential treatment settings, dysfunctional families, and substandard living environments. Once labeled as a criminal or learning-disabled person (i.e., juvenile delinquent, sex offender, retarded, learning disabled, etc.) the more likely it is for the patient to learn and live that label (role).

[9] John Bergman. Drama Therapy for Youth Workshop. September 7, 2001; Radisson Hotel, North Charleston, S.C.

Punitive responses to crime and particularly incarceration (or secure residential treatment) tend to emphasize one role in the person to the detriment of all others. A youth detention sentence (or residential treatment) and the secure facility regime (program milieu) encourage a person to play the role of prisoner (patient) and criminal (offender/delinquent) twenty-four hours a day as opposed to student, son, daughter, friend, peer, athlete, etc. (Thompson, J., 1999).

When we design programs that have fixed, institutionalized standards of behavior, we very easily encourage the attributes that we are trying to avoid. Teaching a fixed standard of behavior encourages further fixed or rigid thinking and behaving (living the life of a patient with rules and regulations that do not parallel life in the greater community). Teaching a fixed standard of behavior attempts to replace one set of concrete behaviors with another and therefore does not challenge the core problems that are the stereotypical responses to social problems (Thompson, J. 1999).

In summary, we have found that the use of experiential treatment can play a critical role in the effective treatment of youth, as a counter balance to traditional techniques. While serious sit-down therapy in the form of individual, family, and group treatment, and psycho-educational classes are essential to any treatment process, such treatment/therapy has its limitations. To enhance the youthful patients' learning and personal growth, we encourage you to move beyond traditional methods. In addition to group, family, and individual therapy, we encourage the use of a wide range of treatments and modalities with youth including the use of experiential treatment.

CHAPTER TWO

GUIDELINES AND PRINCIPLES FOR USING EXPERIENTIAL TREATMENTS

There are several basic guidelines and principles to take into account when using experiential therapies. As exciting as this work can be, one must use caution and keep in mind the well being of the patient. Experiential treatment can move the patient more quickly and in different ways than traditional talk therapies. An experienced clinician using experiential therapies can enhance treatment by helping provide opportunities for insights to patient learning, and making the overall treatment experience more attractive and interesting. The challenge for experiential treatment providers is to offer the opportunity for patients to learn without telling patients what to do and how to do it, what to think, and what to feel, or in other words, doing treatment for them.

Verbal/linguistic-based cognitive-behavioral treatment models and treatment methods dominate the world of programs treating youth and adolescents. They are effective when they address distorted thinking, empathy, perspective taking, cognitive restructuring, and decision-making. Methods include psycho-education, social and life skills development, competency skills building, and coping skills. All programming should try to match the cognitive skills of the patient and be delivered by staff that are committed to the program, program philosophy, and process, and competent to do the work. Treatment should be based upon the stages of development through which youth are likely to progress. Experiential treatments can be used in conjunction with most cognitive behavioral treatment modalities and models that address empathy, anger management, perspective taking, cognitive restructuring, decision-making, education, life skills development, and interventions for problems experienced by the patient.

Many patients are often diagnosed with attachment disorder, oppositional defiant disorder, and have severe behavioral problems. The patients' behavioral responses to situations are typically learned and strengthened through frequent repetition. They are automatic responses (often not thought out) to social and other situations. Learned behavior is closely connected to doing experiential work. Both are composed of definitions of performance and imply a learning of roles. When using experiential treatments, we do not exclude the basic cognitive-behavioral treatments used in most residential and community-based programs, but rather work in conjunction with them to enhance them.

Two important concepts within cognitive-behavioral treatment that are closely linked to experiential learning processes are role reversal and perspective taking. The emphasis on role reversal is familiar to most therapists who see the value in having a patient switch roles with another person; usually a significant person in the patient's life, i.e., a father, mother, sibling, close friend, teacher, etc., with whom they have an unresolved conflict. Playing relevant roles facilitates the patient's learning and skills development while engaging him/her in perspective taking and, in some cases, empathic roles. The active representation and exploration of his/her own life is essential to good treatment (Bergman, 2001).

New behavior is not learned by describing it or telling someone about it. It becomes incorporated into one's life by re-enactment, rehearsal (practice), which is a vital part of the process. One of the foundations in this work is to have the patient look critically at his/her own behavior. Behavior does not occur in a vacuum. Where there is behavior, there are thoughts (cognitions) and feelings (emotions) guiding it (Longo, R.E., 2001).

Programs and patients need to develop cognitive dexterity. Cognitive dexterity is the <u>ability</u> of individuals to look at all possibilities and situations, and to be able to read different (multiple) rather than singular meanings. Patients need the ability to be able to respond to situations in a variety of ways, and to explore different ways of learning and thinking. Cognitive dexterity also refers to a mental <u>ability</u> that is open, flexible, and able to generate realistic solutions to complex problems. It defies rigid thinking and prioritizes flexibility and spontaneity. Insisting on a right way (single way), limits this ability and inhibits the development of a mentally dextrous approach to social interactions and life problems. Learning to weigh all of the possible perspectives encourages standing in another's shoes before actions are taken (perspective taking and empathy). Experiential treatments provide opportunities for patients to learn through one or more of the multiple intelligences they typically use.

One cannot hope for personal change if the teaching style treats patients as objects to be filled with correct ways of thinking and behaving. In encouraging people to become healthy and develop a healthy self, we cannot have a pre-scripted idea of where they are or should be going. We hope you will find as much excitement in doing this work as we have over the years and continue to experience when we work with children.

Using Experiential Exercises

There are several basic principles one is encouraged to follow in using experiential treatments with youth. This work does not require anything more than your time and a willingness to experiment and be creative. The basic principles for this work are summarized below.

1. *Staff training and experience.* Before using experiential exercises in treatment, all staff working with the patient population need to be properly trained. They should be trained in the basic principles and philosophy of the program; trained in the area of child development; trained in the area of specialty that the program is designed for, i.e., child with behavioral problems, children with sexual problems, and then trained in using experiential exercises.

2. *Be creative.* The second basic principle is that the facilitator (leader, clinician, trainer) of experiential exercises must feel comfortable being creative. Not everyone is comfortable standing up before a group and engaging in the exercises that follow. Some people may have a discomfort about the use of touch (see Appendix A), some may have physical limitations, and others may simply be embarrassed to engage is this type of work. You need to be sensitive to your level of comfort with these activities. If you are not willing to participate in them, it may be best that you not facilitate them.

3. *Do not go into this work with expectations of successful outcomes.* Often times, in the midst of these concerns, we place expectations on ourselves that what we do be perfect. This is not the case with experiential exercises. If you are using creative process you must be prepared to succeed as well as expect that sometimes these exercises will simply flop. In this process you will make mistakes and experience failures, and you could easily conclude you're a failure after trying to lead them. Welcome to the club! When doing this work, focus on the process and not particular outcomes. Sometimes an anticipated outcome will occur, while at other times a very different yet positive outcome will emerge. Don't create unrealistic expectations for yourself or for the patients.

4. *It is okay to make mistakes and experience exercise failures.* One cannot predict human behavior, especially with youth. It may take time and several groups using only warm-up exercises to move the patients into a serious mode versus a silly mode. Kids will ham things up just to have fun and be silly. This is okay. Let them have the time to discover, explore, and learn. If an exercise does not work, do not conclude that the exercise is bad or that you are a failure. Try it again another time and move on to a different exercise.

5. *Practice exercises first before using them in clinical or teaching situations.* One way of understanding the exercises and ensuring their success is to practice them by yourself or with other colleagues or friends. Become familiar with them and the potential outcomes. We strongly suggest you do each exercise yourself before you engage patients in doing them.

6. *Spontaneity and creativity are foundations of the work.* Being creative requires the facilitator to be comfortable being spontaneous. In the middle of an exercise it is totally permissible to shift gears and move in a different direction depending upon the process of the group. Remember, we want to avoid rigid thinking and fixed outcomes. Spontaneity and creativity go hand in hand.

7. *Involve all staff and patients.* Experiential exercises require that everyone participate, unless physical limitations, or other disabilities prevent them from doing so. Warm-up exercises are designed to help build comfort in doing this work within individuals. It is a time to learn to work with basic props and kinesis. It is also a time to have fun as the patients learn and become more comfortable with experiential work. Again, this may take some time. Don't rush the process. What is important is that everyone is involved and learns to develop a personal level of comfort in doing the work.

8. *All patients are given the opportunity to work.* We have all had the experience of having patients who are wallflowers, who are quite comfortable not saying or doing anything in group. One of the beauties of experiential work is that it involves everyone. If the patient refuses to participate, the patient can observe and give feedback to others. Certainly, onlookers have their own experience in just watching experiential work.

9. *All material is authentic in the work.* As long as we do not tell patients what to say or what to do, and what to think and feel, the work that results is real and authentic. Even if the patient responds in a nervous (nervous laughter and silly fashion (distracting or avoidant behavior), what we see in the patient is real and authentic, and therefore worthy of the effort. Such reactions can and should be explored with the patient.

10. *Don't tell patients what to think and feel.* One of the essential points in this type of work is to have the patient look critically at his/her own behavior. Programs and their staff need to develop cognitive dexterity by honoring the patients' ability to identify the meaning of their own thoughts and feelings. This leads to patient self-discovery and patients' memory of past events which in turn lead to self-expression and associated thoughts and feelings.

11. *Be careful about telling patients what to do.* As a facilitator or clinician we have to take charge over a variety of issues including the patients safety, the safety of others, and maintaining a safe environment. These exercises require that participants be given directions for each exercise and how to follow them. It is the nature of how we ask others to do things that matters. Aggressive and/or controlling patients don't like being told what to do. Encourage and support them without being overbearing and overly controlling/directive. This work is about behavioral change not behavioral control. The goal of the work is to teach patients self-control, not how to respond to staff control. We don't want participants to react to or act out in response to this work, but rather to respond to the situations we create in doing experiential work. The goal is for patients to understand the whys, hows, and benefits of visual/spatial, kinetic, and language-based treatment.

One final note here. In working with youth we often (consciously or subconsciously) tend to push youth into traditional gender roles (Bergman, J. 2001; Robinson, S. L. 2002). For example, male roles include be strong, silent, in control, independent, and not giving the appearance of looking weak. For females the traditional roles are being dependent, not questioning, focus on beauty and appearance, and not appearing to be smart. If we hope to effect change in young people we work with it is important to break down the barriers that support the gender roles they may use to avoid doing in-depth work.

Engaging Patients in Experiential Treatments and Exercises

When beginning this work with patients it is important that you start with warm-up exercises. Patients need to become comfortable with these most basic and fun activities before moving them into introductory and then more advanced exercises. Warm-up exercises should include activities that help patients explore and gradually learn to be comfortable with thoughts, words, movement, and touch while enjoying the exercises. These exercises are also important in building group cohesion, cooperation, trust between patients, and trust between patients and staff. The process for engaging patients in experiential treatments requires the following principles.

1. *Start with a relaxation exercise.* Relaxation helps people get focused. In addition relaxation helps people move to the creative side of thinking. Before engaging patient's in exercises, we encourage you to do a few minutes of relaxation. Combining relaxation with pleasant guided imagery further engages the creative thought process.

2. *Identify the patient's strengths.* Patients will benefit most from treatment and especially from experiential work when we help them identify their personal strengths. Once identified, professionals can then help patients build upon and expand their personal strengths.

3. *Explain the exercise to the patients.* It is important to explain the exercise to patients. Get their permission (use informed consent if necessary) to participate and address immediately any concerns or reluctance.

4. *The patient must have the physical and emotional skills to understand the exercise.* It is essential that the patient has the physical and emotional skills to understand what is going on and what the work is about. If you are working with younger children, make sure the exercises are modified to work with their level of understanding and psychomotor ability. Keep in mind the patients' learning style.

5. *Work in the here and now. It is important to work in the present; the here and now.* Even when addressing past events the work the patient does should be focused on intrapersonal processes in the "here and now". For example, when working on past events suggest to the patient that she/he experience it now with leading statements such as, "imagine you are in that situation now; describe the environment, naming who is present, and what you are doing now." Avoid participants describing the past. Rather, have them describe what they want and need in the here and now.

6. *The patient must have ultimate control.* The patient must able to make a safe place in his/her head in case he/she needs to go there (Bergman, J. 2001). A safe place can be anyplace or anything in terms of a mental image that gives the patient a sense of safety and comfort. The patient has total control of his or her safe place and determines who can be there with him or her and who can not. If the patient wants to stop the exercise, honor the patient's request to do so.

7. *The patient understands that he/she can STOP the exercise at any time.* It is critical that the patient understands that he/she can STOP the exercise at any time; that he/she is in control, not the facilitator. There should never be a consequence to a patient for not participating in or stopping an exercise once it has begun.

Types of Exercises

When one looks at general and basic programming in treatment programs for youth, there are several core treatment areas to be addressed. These areas of treatment often focus on anger management, cognitive restructuring, emotional development, social and interpersonal skills building, values clarification, personal abuse and victimization issues, healthy boundaries, self-esteem building, and the use of coping responses and interventions to correct problematic behavior, among others. There are several types of exercises one can use to incorporate experiential work into the treatment process with children and adolescents who have a variety of behavioral problems (Longo, 2002). They include but are not limited to the following:

- The Three Ts
  - team building
  - trust
  - touch

Many of the exercises that focus on any one of the Three Ts skills usually incorporate the others, e.g., team buildin requires trust and touch is often a part of many trust building exercises, which often require touch. Many of the Thre Ts require patients to communicate in order to complete the exercise, which helps them work with words and language

- Exercises that work with words and language focus on:
  - self-expression
  - self-exploration
  - self-disclosure

Many exercises that build the patient's comfort in talking and relating to others additionally focus on self-expression self-exploration, and self-disclosure. These exercises also focus on cognitive restructuring.

- Exercises that work with cognitive restructuring focus on:
  - self-awareness
  - interpersonal skills
  - intrapersonal skills
  - self-esteem building

Cognitive distortions usually impact interpersonal relationships in a negative way. Exercises that focus on cognitiv restructuring also help facilitate stronger relationships. Healthy relationships require healthy emotional expression Cognitive distortions directly effect the patient's ability to recognize and express emotions.

- Exercises that work with emotional development and expression focus on:
  - identification and recognition of feelings
  - empathy development

These exercises also focus on personal victimization and personal abuse work which are often linked to the patient anger and problematic behaviors. Child abuse and neglect, when undetected or untreated are often associated wit behavioral acting out.

- Exercises that work with behavioral issues focus on:
  - anger management
  - assertiveness training

Exercises that focus on managing behavior also facilitate working with cognitive restructuring and emotional manage ment, which in turn address the patient's core values and beliefs.

- Exercises that work with values clarification and personal beliefs focus on:
  - healthy boundaries

As the patient works with his/her core values and beliefs and healthy boundaries, their social skills and competenc skills are usually enhanced.

- Exercises that work with skills building focus on:
  - social competencies
  - social skills
  - peer relations

WARM UP EXERCISES

As we noted above, this work should always begin with warm-up exercises until the group has had several opportunities to practice basic skills in order to move to more advanced work. When first starting out it is important to "warm" patients up to the more intensive and possibly intrusive work they will do in treatment. Experiential work should build on previous work done by the patient and/or the group.

In order to begin doing this work we recommend that you start groups with warm-up exercises (often referred to as "Icebreakers" (Sue Forbess-Greene, L.M.S.W.). Warm-up exercises are used to get people focused on the group and its activities, to get their energy flowing (kinesis), and are also used to get the group to relax. They lighten the atmosphere, and energize tired, low-energy individuals. They help reduce anxiety while bringing the group together (team work) and finally engage mind **and** body. Warm-ups and introductory level exercises should be enjoyable and include exercises that help patients explore and learn to gradually be comfortable with thoughts, words, movement, and touch while enjoying them. These exercise are also important in building group cohesion and trust between patients and trust between patients and staff. These exercises should be fun.

EXERCISES INVOLVING TOUCH (PHYSICAL CONTACT)

Not all patients enjoy or welcome personal or physical contact. Something as simple as a handshake can trigger traumatic feelings and something as harmless as a quick hug can result in the patient sexualizing your relationship with him or her. In this book are several warm-up exercises that will help patients explore basic issues regarding boundaries and personal touch concerns. Physical contact (touching another) can lead to the most serious of all boundary violations whether it is physical aggression or sexually inappropriate behavior. Therefore when doing these exercises it is important to have two or more staff persons present so one can monitor the group and its activities.

Touch is a major part of many experiential exercises. When we get participants to touch "something" or "somebody" it opens up methods to assess a person's boundaries. The work needs to proceed cautiously and slowly with those who have been victimized. Victims get pushed into hidden (secret) places, small places and victims are held down.

In Appendix A of this book are guidelines for the use of touch developed for New Hope Treatment Centers. These guidelines can serve as a guide for doing experiential exercises as well as for establishing policy within your program for the use of touch. Remember, Appendix A is only to serve as a guide, not policy. Programs must develop their own policy regarding the use of touch between patients and between patients and staff.

IN THE BEGINNING

All exercises that are used within a group or a gathering of people should be selected at the facilitator's discretion, including the warm-up exercises. Therefore, it is important that the facilitator be familiar with participants (patients/staff) and their issues/problems. The facilitator should instruct participants that the exercises are to be taken seriously and that they should be sensitive to the level of personal sharing that may occur by other participants during any one particular exercise.

DEBRIEFING

It should be anticipated that participants will feel they have learned more about themselves and learned something about others in the group after participating in many of these exercises. Even warm-up exercises offer the potential for significant personal learning. Most of the exercises in this book include a list of process (debriefing) questions the facilitator can use to process the exercise with participants. If there are not specific process questions at the end of a particular exercise, then the following questions can be used to help facilitate discussion about any of the exercises and helping patients explore personal/individual experiences. After each exercise the facilitator should discuss/process the exercise with participants. Suggested questions include:

What was fun about this exercise?
What was hard about this exercise?
What did you learn about yourself?
What did you learn about others in the group?
How will you work with differences between yourself and others?
How might what you learned effect the work you do or your being in treatment?
How can you use what you learned from this exercise to work better with others?
What thoughts came to mind when you were doing this exercise?
What feelings did you experience when doing this exercise?

INTRODUCTORY LEVEL EXERCISES

Introductory level exercises are the next step in doing experiential work. They should be used after participants have had the opportunity to work with many of the warm-up exercises.

Introductory level exercises are still fun and educational but they turn the heat up a level. In other words, as the heat goes up, the intensity, seriousness, and potential therapeutic benefit from the exercise increases. As with all exercises, these should be debriefed and discussed with process/follow-up questions. Some of these exercises will have "YES" in the *cautions* category of the exercise, as they can open up personal issues that may need to be further addressed after the exercise as well as in future therapy groups or sessions. Most of these exercises, like the warm-ups, explore basic areas of trust, movement and touch, feelings and emotions, and one's cognitive process.

INTERMEDIATE LEVEL EXERCISES

Intermediate level exercises should generally follow when a group has done some of the introductory level exercises that explore similar themes and issues, i.e., trust, personal disclosure, etc. While many of these exercises are fun and educational they turn up the heat even more than do the introductory level exercises. Again, after each exercise it is important to allow time to debrief, discuss, and process the exercise. Most of these exercises will have a "YES" in the *cautions* category, as they are designed to facilitate personal exploration and can open up issues that will often need follow-up work. Most of these exercises, like the warm-ups and introductory level exercises, explore issues related to trust, self-disclosure, feelings and emotions, and one's cognitive process.

ADVANCED LEVEL EXERCISES

Advanced exercises are designed to have therapeutic value for those who participate in them. The facilitator should be well versed in doing experiential work or work with another professional who is experienced in working with participants at a therapeutic level. There are a variety of exercises in this category that include various techniques that are described in more detail below.

ROLE-PLAY

Role-plays are a common type of experiential exercise used in group therapy and in individual therapy sessions. Role-plays are done by identifying problematic situations, discussing different types and/or cycles of behavior in the problematic situations, confronting the distorted thinking that may occur in those situations (i.e., one's view of certain incidents or relationships), and then planning for the future. The process for both scripted and improvised role-play can be very similar to life issues talked about in treatment. Role-plays might also include aspects of personal role development, plot/narrative creation, exploring conflicts, and practicing resolution of conflicts and rehearsal of new skills. Role-plays can therefore undermine fixed "personal" characteristics and "acting-out" behavior by offering new character roles to explore and new kinds of behavior to practice (Thompson, J., 1999).

BEGINNING EXPERIENTIAL EXERCISES

There is often a natural resistance by people to engage in this type of treatment as they are doing "it" in front of others. This work brings the real world into the treatment session and for some it can be very shame inducing, embarrassing, and difficult. The facilitator should anticipate this and be ready to discuss patients' concerns and anticipation of what is going to happen. This the importance of beginning with warm-up exercises. The facilitator(s) needs to be observant of all those in the group and constantly be looking everywhere in order to see what affect is going on with particular group members. Again, this is why it is important to have other staff present, when possible, while doing experiential work. John Bergman and Saul Hewish of Geese Theatre Company (1996), note there are three levels of function to be addressed before beginning experiential work.

THE FIRST LEVEL OF FUNCTION

The first level of function is to *get the participants physically moving*, which begins to open up physical and kinetic memory, something that talk therapy alone may not do, or do well for some patients. A simple physical stance can generate a variety of affect. For example, if the facilitator simply walked over to a corner of the room and stood in the corner with his back to the room and his head down in a sulking position, imagine the physical memories and imagination in the group members that might be stirred up.

As a facilitator, one must have an idea about what it is you're trying to get the participants to do. Is this a new group that does not know or trust each other? What is the affect you are going for in the group? With warm-up and introductory level exercises you are not always looking for a catharsis, although some patients may experience such. If the group or several individuals offer resistance, ask what is it like to feel that feeling of resistance. Engage them in simple exercises that might get them to experience the feeling of resistance. Use an exercise that has a sense of focus and purpose. For example, Exercise W,I -32 Words and Phrases might be a way to explore resistance.

Warm-up exercises have specific goals:
1. To get the patients working together (The Three Ts).
2. To get the patent thinking and working cognitively.
2. To help patients become comfortable with physical exercises (moving one's body, The Three Ts).

Physical exercises (movement) help people discover their sense of success with doing and accomplishing tasks. There is no other psychological intent. These exercises simply get them to use their bodies and work together as a group.

THE SECOND LEVEL OF FUNCTION

Bergman and Hewish (1996), note that the second level of function is designed to *help the patient function on a physical and mental level*. They initiate group and cognitive skills. The second level of function also helps build a team framework while developing trust. The facilitator should pay close attention to the exercises that focus on these issues to see what happens. Some patients do not cooperate initially and this effects trust building and team building. Look for strategies of cooperation, resistance, leadership, and coping among participants. Take the time to explore participant's reactions to these exercises by using process questions. Explore thoughts, feelings, memories, resistance, and what the experience was like for each patient to participate in the exercises.

We have found in conducting training for professionals that an exercise like Blind Walk/Blind Circle (Exercise W-3) opens up a variety of issues even for the most seasoned professional. What was it like to walk with your eyes closed and rely on others? Who opened their eyes? And why? Self-trust and trust of others are common concerns. Women often fear being touched in sexual ways by males, thus trust of the opposite sex may be an issue.

THE THIRD LEVEL OF FUNCTION

The third level of function is designed to help the participants focus on their affect (emotions) and the activity of the imagination (thinking). Bergman and Hewish (1996) report that when one gets to this level, the hope is to begin getting some glimpses at the patient's private/secret world. This is more likely to occur as you get into the intermediate and advanced exercises. It is not uncommon, however, to witness this phenomenon happen with introductory level exercises and in some cases even in warm-ups. Exercise A-1 Personas, is an exercise specifically designed to work with the patient's secret/private self.

When doing work in groups, it is important that the group open with warm-up exercises before moving into introductory and more advanced exercises. As the facilitator turns up the heat in exercises or moves toward more advanced exercises, the goal is to work toward addressing the main treatment issues for a particular patient or for the entire group.

After the group has engaged in experiential work, allow time for the group to process the work. The facilitator should set aside enough time to work toward pre-closure of the group (addressing individual and group concerns/issues) and then toward final closure of the group. At times individual or group follow-up may be necessary. Know the patient(s) well and anticipate possible outcomes without controlling for or creating specific outcomes.

GUIDELINES FOR ROLE-PLAY AND DRAMA THERAPY

"Drama therapy has a beginning, middle and end. It is a story retold, rediscovered, or imagined that makes a person have solutions."

~ *John Bergman*

Role-play, mime, human still photos, and human sculptures are all forms of drama therapy. The use of drama therapy exercises with patients can 1) enhance treatment by offering new and different insight to patient learning, and 2) enrich the overall treatment experience. As noted above the challenge for facilitators, clinicians and others using experiential exercises and drama exercises is to offer the opportunity for patients and the facilitator to learn together without teaching (telling) patients a "correct way" to behave/react/respond to the exercises. One does not want to micro manage/direct role-plays and experiential exercises to the point that creativity and spontaneity are lost.

We noted earlier that behaviors/responses to certain situations are learned and strengthened through frequent and often daily rehearsal. These learned behaviors are well ingrained in the person's repertoire of social interactions and life situations. The same process applies to trauma.

Traumatized patients often develop fixed and rigid patterns of behavior in response to stressful situations and trauma. Many of the youth clinicians work with have experienced some type of trauma and may suffer from PTSD. Trauma is often stored in muscle memory and thus accessed through somatic experiences and exercises involving movement.

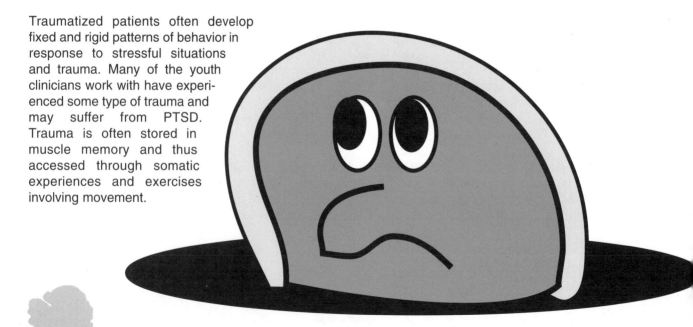

o access these areas for treatment purposes, we noted before that we must offer patients the freedom to work without staff controlling the patient or over-controlling the work/therapeutic process. In doing so we must also attend to the traditional gender roles we observe in our patients. For example, the traditional male role is often pushed in treatment, and thus we see male patients who act like the strong silent type. This was the case in a recent group where one of our patients was asked to describe his private self (secret persona) through selecting one of several masks and then use flash cards to describe the feelings and thoughts associated with the mask. In reporting to the group he stated he selected the silly mask as that was a part he seldom shows in treatment. He noted, "I am told by peers and staff that I am too serious and act like an old man." He stated he was afraid to reveal the childish part of himself.

Much of what we do in treatment is usually in the box, that is traditional talk therapy. Experiential treatments help us think and work outside the box. Experiential exercises can help the patient move towards some form of cathartic experience. Simple role-plays adhere to the following principles (Bergman & Hewish, 1996):

. Always do warm-up exercises to start the work.
. Focus on using a single cognitive process (one performed by the patient).
. Use a simple, single process. This work should not be complex in design; use
  only one conflict.
. Use two people.
. Any affect will do (never tell the patient what to feel).

One concern we need to mention is that many of our patients are very inept at putting out their true thoughts and feelings. Program rules that prohibit the use of profanity often result in the patient "filtering" their true thoughts and feelings with talk therapy as well as in experiential work. An angry, assaultive child who is on the verge of acting-out is not thinking: "you really upset me and I need to give you a piece of my mind." Instead he or she is most likely thinking, "F- -k you, who the hell do you think you are, telling me what to do. I'm gonna kick you're a - -!"

Our experience is that angry patients have angry violent thoughts that they try to conceal so they "look good" in treatment. Therefore when patients are in group and using role-plays and other experiential exercises, we encourage the true self to emerge and we tell them that for purposes of self-expression (while in group) they are allowed to use the actual thoughts and feelings they are experiencing. We waive the program rules about profane language.

Role-plays can be used to help patients and others use the coping skills they need in day-to-day life, from moment to moment. It gives us a glimpse at how they present answers and coping skills in the real world. Thus, role-plays are tools we can use to help patients rehearse their lives.

DRAMA THERAPY

Drama therapy takes role-play a step further, and the work can become more intense. Bergman & Hewish (1996) note that drama therapy has a beginning, middle, and an end. It is a story retold, discovered, or imagined that helps the person work toward solutions.

Drama therapy is designed to go beyond traditional sit down talk therapy. Drama therapy becomes a tool that clinicians and facilitators can use to reach for affect and feelings because it quickly engages the person in an experience. Drama therapy deals with the complexity of thoughts, memories, fear, anxiety and the vast array of all other feelings in a present-centered moment. It takes time and practice to master, and should not be done without adequate and specialized training. Bergman (2001) notes, "Drama therapy can lead to a place where old terrors become real and present. "

One form of drama work is the use of mime to open up memories and activate feelings. Simple mime can be extremely powerful in generating affect. Watching mime, especially when accompanied by a well suited piece of music in the background, helps patients take on a role from their past experience. Again, Bergman (2001) notes, "It is not a haphazard art form, but rather a precise therapy used in moving people to an affective level."

When using experiential treatments (and in particular, when we use these therapeutically to work with particular problems), it is important to look for the small details of the person's behavior. Often these behaviors and problems are associated with guilt and/or shame and are held in secret. Experiential work is useful in breaking open the patient's private/secret world by initiating different types of affect. The work creates an experience to which the patient has some form of reaction.

In role-play and drama work, one goal is to identify critical experiences for the patient, i.e., feeling vulnerable, or contacting or connecting with anger and/or rage the patient doesn't usually acknowledge. We want to create an experience to initiate the patient's reaction. In doing so we want to explore the patient's imagination and fantasy world that leads toward these feelings. The experience helps us see how the patient responds (his/her way of being) and the cognitive strategies he/she uses to cope with the problem and/or feelings. When the patient is engaged, we see his/her inner imagination, and a picture of the world in which he/she lives.

Bergman & Hewish (1996) note, when the interior landscape (what happens inside the person's head) is revealed, it offers us a broad understanding of ways we can then work with the patient. To understand the concept of the interior landscape we attempt to engage the patient's thought process: "what is it like to be small", "what is it like to feel weak and defenseless", "what is it like to have a sense of no control of the world around you". The clinician tries to understand what it must be like for the patient in order to make him/her self feel safe.

Once the patient goes to a safe place, find out where he/she has gone to... in his mind, i.e., under bed, a special room, a certain place. Ask the patient what he/she feels, what she/he is afraid of, what it is like to be afraid. If afraid of a person then ask what the person he/she fears is like, etc. Inside the safe place is where all the outside tapes come in. i.e., it's not fair, not right. Deviant tapes are also there.

Drama therapy is advanced work and we suggest you familiarize yourself with the literature in order to do the best work you can with your patients.

TOOLS TO WORK WITH

Several of the exercises in this book may call for specific materials. Most of these materials are readily available. One does not need a lot to get started. With role-plays and drama work just having an empty chair and a doorway as props can lead to a lot of experiential work (Bergman & Hewish, 1996).

There are a variety of "props" one can use to enhance experiential work. Props that have sounds, smells, and/or convey feelings (such as masks) can be used and may also serve as metaphors, i.e. something evil or awful. Other props such as dolls, puppets, toys, masks, art supplies, and a variety of gizmos can be slowly collected. One can use one's children's toys as they outgrow them, shop at garage sales, or go to toy and specialty stores to build a collection of props. As you work with props, display them prominently for the patients to see. It is fine for the patients or participants to look at, touch, and explore props that are put out on the floor or a table.

No matter where you work, there are generally basic props that are always available. Work with what is there, you don't need a lot. Doors, chairs, and floors are a good start. Using a door allows the participant to get in and to leave, to come or go, and to escape, for example see Exercise W,I –29, Through the Door.. Using a chair can also be a very powerful tool. Sitting in an empty chair can be anyone the client wants to speak to. Using the floor can serve as a means to fall to it or go through it into any world. It can be a place to hide while walls and corners are places to feel strong (Bergman and Hewish, (1996).

ROPS AND MASKS

rops can help raise the heat and the affect in a particular exercise, i.e., a high heel shoe on a chair. With a high heel hoe on a chair we can explore; Who is She? Where did she come from? Did you stalk her? What are you feeling? What is she feeling? Where are you now? Where were you? To test the power of a prop, simply ask the patient, "What o you remember when you look at it?

Masks are also very powerful props. Use masks to make still photos, in mime, or in role-plays. Ask questions about who, where, what's going on? What is the person feeling? Have you ever felt that way? Let the patients use their imagination and association. Have the patient wear a mask that represents what they are like when they are about to ecome angry, depressed, withdraw, do something horrible, etc. Hold up another mask and ask how the patient goes rom this mask to that mask, and what are the steps in the process. A brief out line on the historical use of masks and asic mask construction can be found in Appendix B.

Dolls are also valuable props. Put a doll on a chair when starting a session and see what happens. Ask them about he doll. Who is it? How old is he/she? Where is he/she?

MUSIC

A lot of the work we do is done with music. Research on music and its effect on people has shown that hearing music an have a healing effect and can serve as a trigger of memories, thoughts and feelings. Music can alter the mood of room. We have all had the experience of a "favorite song" that brings us back to a positive memory, or watching a cene in a movie where the background music makes us well up with feelings and emotions. We prefer to use music without lyrics in most of our work, however, if you use music with lyrics, know that lyrics will usually guide the thought rocess. Make sure the lyrics address the central theme you are working with in the group. Music without lyrics lets articipants go where they want without guidance or can be used to guide them to a particular place, i.e., draw your amily, draw a safe place, etc.

PERSONAL VICTIMIZATION AND VICTIM EMPATHY WORK

When one has been abused, it is likely that there will be a variety of issues to be addressed in the treatment process. Part of working with personal victimization is to get in touch with affect and empathy. Many abused persons do not have empathy for themselves, which translates into not having empathy for others. This s especially true with patients who have both been abused and then act-out abu-sively toward others. It is likely that working with these issues through role-play and drama work will result in the person having a cathartic experience. Often, the difficulty as well as the success in doing this work is finding methods that get to the inner rage and fears the patient experiences.

One technique in developing empathy with role-play is to have the patient become their "victim" and experience the belief and behavior of he other as well as experience the physical, psychological, and emo-ional pieces as much as possible. Teaching empathy is a four-step process (Bays and Longo, 2000).

First, we have to teach patients how to recognize emotions and feelings.

Second, we help them to the point of being able to look at the victim's perspec-ive.

The third step is assisting the person in replicating the feelings and emo-ions of others.

The fourth step is exploring with the patient their response decision; that is, how they will choose to respond to the process of putting his/her self in someone else's shoes. This is often a difficult step for many people. It is easier to avoid or otherwise challenge another's thoughts, feelings, and situation than to put one's self into it.

To develop empathy with role-play is to have the patient become the other person and experience the belief and behavior of the other as well as experience the physical and emotional pieces as much as possible.

Role-play and drama work can be done in several ways. Role-plays can involve the victim, the victimizer, a bystander, or any combination of these roles or others. Role-plays can involve families, peers, intimates, and others in the patient's social circle. The goal is to make an experience so there can be a reaction. Some further guidelines and pitfalls in this work include the following: A) Do *not* pay too much attention to the strategies the patient uses to avoid affect. If you do this you may end up playing right into the patient's resistance. B) The clinician needs to have confidence in him/her self in doing this work. This type of work does not always succeed. A hunch or idea may be tried and fail. It is okay to fail or make a fool of yourself once in a while. With experiential work we cannot always know what will happen nor can we predict the outcome of these exercises. Keep focused on the treatment objectives for the patient. Is he/she reaching them or not?

ACTING OUT BEHAVIOR

When working with patients who act-out, our goal is to see the connection of thoughts and feelings that lead to acting-out behavior. Once we help the patients identify thoughts and feelings we can help them find both thought and feeling substitutes. This happens when they begin to seriously work on changing thoughts and feelings that lead to acting out behaviors. In training and working with other programs we have found that many professionals pay very little attention to what it is the patients are experiencing in the world. When we work with affect, we take the time to go back and discuss/process what the patient is doing in his/her head. In that regard, Bergman (2001) notes,

> "Catharsis on its own is not enough. We have to go to the secret strategies, etc. that lead to aggressive and assaultive behavior. Therefore we need to explore the details of these assaults. Inside the smallest details lies the fuel for the aggression and/or deviance, and thus we need to ask the patient for details. For example, with a sexually aggressive patient we might ask, 'when did you take out your penis, was it erect, how aroused were you, what were you feeling and thinking right then?' This type of work builds on itself and we cannot skip critical steps of the work."

Bergman and Hewish (1996) note that role-play and drama work can be used to work with the following treatment areas:

The Hiding Place. The hiding place is a safe place. It is a metaphor for where the person hides in his/her head; a place where the person retreats to feel safe and secure. Often one can do exercises (described later) that have participants draw a safe place. When done with music, it can be a powerful and insightful means of learning for both the patient and clinician.

High Risk Role Work. When working with anyone, there are situations and internal dilemmas that represent risks to the individual's personal, physical and psychological safety and with aggressive patients, the safety of others. High risk role work involves role-plays and drama work that brings out those risks and helps the individual deal with methods of coping, behavioral alternatives, and new ways of thinking, feeling, and behaving regarding those risks.

High Risk Role Simulation. In more advanced stages of role-play and drama work we use high risk role simulation. This type of experiential work is where the clinician is able to see if patients have learned what we have been teaching them. With this type of exercise the goals are to continue to develop patient skills and help them better understand their *Cognitive Wheel* (cycle). For example, if we look at aggressive youth, a cognitive wheel might look like this:

1. I feel humiliated at school
2. I go home after school and brood/sulk
3. I think, feel and sense it (life, school, parents, etc.) is unfair
4. I have thoughts of revenge
5. I have a fantasy of revenge (patients break rules enters an unsafe place)
6. I act out (whatever behavior, sexual assault, assault)
7. I make a false apology with guilt to never do it again
8. I set myself up to do it all over again

Role-plays and drama work are useful methods of taking a patient into an experience or situation that makes him angry, very dangerous, and can help him find a strategy that helps him/her control it. Rehearsal is important. Role-plays and drama work that are used to help patients rehearse a replacement behavior are critical. In experiential work think of role-plays as the practice sessions the professional athletes do before they go out to play in a real game or competition. Practice, practice, practice is important! The role-play should focus on one part of the cognitive wheel, whereby the patient rehearses each part until he/she can feel successful in the intervention. The patient does it over and over again until he/she feels inoculated against the danger of that situation. Bergman (2001) notes,

> "Continue to rehearse and raise the heat. In role-play, as you rehearse, something new is going to occur. When a patient breaks the process ask her/him where she/he went. What did she/he do and what will she/he end up doing in real life? What are the thoughts and feelings that occur when she/he is about to lose it? Where do the thoughts and feelings lead to? What life experience(s) is triggered?"

In summary, it is important to understand the guidelines and principles reviewed in the first two chapters of this book before engaging in experiential work. Child development and working with children with several problems, i.e., RAD, PTSD, Oppositional Defiant Disorder, etc. require an understanding of not only child development but the disorders themselves.

The basic principles outlined in the beginning of this book will help get you on your way to doing basic experiential work. We hope you will enjoy using the following exercises and seeing the changes in your patients.

CHAPTER THREE ~ WARM-UP EXERCISES

EXERCISE W - 1 · MONSTER LEGS

The purpose of this exercise is to build group trust, learn teamwork, and facilitate comfort with touch (Three Ts). Participants are dependent upon each other to complete the exercise. This exercise is a spin-off of the three legged race.

In a large open space or outdoors, participants are asked to stand in a straight line. Each participant has his/her left leg tied to the person's (next to him/her on the left) right leg and the participant's right leg tied to the person's (next to him/her on the right) left leg. Only the participants on each end of the line has a free (unbound) leg. The facilitator ties each pair of legs together with a strip of cloth or two bandanas tied together. The participants are given instructions for movement. For example they are told to walk like a clock hand forward around a tree or stationary object, to walk backwards, to walk to one side and then the other side. Have them form a circle and tie the two legs of the end participants together. Once in the circle have them walk forwards, backwards, and sideways.

VARIATION:

Repeat the same exercise asking some or all participants to close their eyes and keep them closed, or use blind folds for all or some members. They are instructed to follow the voice and instructions of the facilitator.

One of the participants is given the task to be the facilitator and instruct the group where and how to move.

Purpose	Three Ts. Builds comfort with movement.
Level	**W**
Group size	**LG, SG**
Time ~ in minutes	5-10
Materials needed	Bandanas or 3 foot long cloth strips
Cautions	Use an open space free of obstacles to bump into or fall on. Best done outside or on carpeted surface. **PAL = H**
Variations	**Yes**
Process questions	Basic

EXERCISE W - 2 · LEAST NUMBER OF STEPS:

The purpose of this exercise is to build trust, team work, group cohesion, and become comfortable with movement and touch.

Each participant is instructed to go across the room, one at a time, using the least number of steps. Large walking steps, glides, or running is permitted.

VARIATIONS:

Shortest number of trips (the person trips him/herself across the room – simulating a tripping motion), or the shortest number of hops, or the shortest number of skips, or the shortest number of jumps.

Teams Using two people, as a team, cross the room using the shortest number of steps via piggyback (one person on the back of another), hops (with one person's right leg and the other person's left leg tied together with a bandana or cloth strip), skips (with one person's right leg and the other person's left leg tied together with a bandana or cloth strip), jumps (with one person's right leg and the other person's left leg tied together with a bandana or cloth strip).

Purpose	Three Ts. Builds comfort with movement.
Level	**W**
Group size	**LG, SG, P, IC**
Time ~ in minutes	30 seconds to one minute per person or pair
Materials needed	Bandanas or 3 foot long cloth strips
Cautions	Clear room of furniture or sharp/pointed objects, **PAL = H**
Variations	**Yes**
Process questions	Basic

Source: Adapted from John Bergman, Geese Theatre Company.

EXERCISE W - 3 · BLIND WALK

The purpose of this exercise is to have the group work together and develop trust of the group and in other participants. The exercise also builds confidence in movement and comfort with touch.

Participants line up in a straight line in an open area. Participants are not allowed to talk. Each person puts one hand on the shoulder of the person in front of him/her and closes his/her eyes. The person first in line open's his/her eyes and at the facilitator's discretion leads the group in line through the area for about 3-4 minutes. The facilitator of the walk, walks slowly and is careful not to lead the line into objects or places where others may trip, fall, or bump into things. The facilitator watches to make sure the line does not break up. After 3-4 minutes of walking the facilitator tells the line to stop and tells everyone to reverse direction in the line and put one hand on the shoulder of the new person in front of him/her. The trust walk is repeated.

It is good to have several spotters who make sure participants don't walk into objects, furniture, etc.

Explore with participants what it was like to participate in the exercise.

VARIATION:

BLIND WALK IN A CIRCLE:

Participants stand up and form a circle in an open area. Participants are not allowed to talk. There should not be more than 1-2 feet (an arms length between people standing in the circle). The facilitator explains that he/she will take one person at a time and have them close their eyes and launch the person slowly to walk across the inside of the circle. When the person reaches the other side, another participant takes that person's shoulders, turns him/her around, and guides the person back across the circle in a different direction (eyes of the person walking remain closed). The facilitator selects another person from the group and, after he/she closes his/her eyes, slowly pushes the person to walk across the circle. The facilitator selects another person from the group and after he/she closes his/her eyes slowly pushes the person to walk across the circle. Each time a person is selected the participants in the circle need to close the gap to insure that no one walks outside of the circle.

The facilitator instructs the group that the group's job is to keep each person safe and not let them bump into each other. If this looks like it is going to happen a person from the group must step into the circle and stop or redirect one of the people walking to avoid a collision and then sets the person walking across the circle again. The facilitator selects another person from the group and after he/she closes his/her eyes slowly pushes the person to walk across the circle. The process is repeated until there are 4-6 people walking blind across the circle at the same time. Once the last person selected has gone across the circle 3-4 times the exercise is stopped and everyone takes their place in the circle.

The exercise is repeated until all participants have had the chance to participate in the blind circle walk.

PROCESS QUESTIONS:

How much did they trust others?
What was it like to have to rely on the person in front of you to guide you safely?
How many opened their eyes, even if only once for a couple of seconds?
What was the sensation of being touched on your shoulder with your eyes closed like for you?
What was the sensation of touching another's shoulder with your eyes closed like for you?

Purpose	Three Ts. Builds comfort with movement.
Level	**W**
Group size	**LG, SG**
Time ~ in minutes	10-15
Materials needed	Large room, Long hallway, or open outdoor area
Cautions	Rooms and areas should be free of furniture, sharp or pointed objects, and items on the groundor floor that participants can trip over. **PAL = M**
Variations	**Yes**
Process questions	**Yes**

Source: Unknown

EXERCISE W - 4 · PULL-UPS

The purpose of this exercise is to build trust, develop teamwork, and facilitate relationships. The exercise also builds comfort with touch and movement.

Two people sit on the floor facing each other. They place their feet against each other's feet. Then they hold and lock hands or wrists. They have to pull each other up into a standing position. When done repeat the exercise adding a third person, feet to feet, locking hands or wrists. Then the group of three tries to pull each other up. Add a fourth, fifth, person etc. until the group can no longer pull each other up. Make sure all participants have a turn.

VARIATION:

Standing up, both participants grab each other's wrists and hold tight. They place their feet about a foot apart and about 3-6 inches away from the other participants' toes. They extend their arms straight and lean back. Then, bending at the knees, they lower each other into a squatting position and then stand up again.

PROCESS QUESTIONS:

What happened as the exercise grew from two people to three, four or more people?
Did anyone emerge as a facilitator for the group?

Purpose	Three Ts. Builds comfort with movement and facilitating relationships.
Level	**W**
Group size	**SG, P**
Time ~ in minutes	1-2 minutes per pull-up
Materials needed	None
Cautions	Clear immediate area of furniture and objects on the floor. **PAL = H**
Variations	**Yes**
Process questions	**Yes**

Source: Unknown

EXERCISE W - 5 · THINGS IN COMMON

The purpose of this exercise is to help participants build trust in others and feel comfortable using words and expressing feelings.

Participants pair off into small groups of 3 or 4. Each group talks about things they have in common as a group, i.e., each is in school, each has a brother/sister, each wears glasses, each likes Italian food, etc.

PROCESS QUESTIONS:

Have group members share those items they found in common.
How did it feel to you when you had similarities?
How did it feel to you when you had differences?
What was hard to share?
What was easy to share?

Purpose	To build trust and comfort with words and feelings.
Level	**W**
Group size	**SG, 3-4**
Time ~ in minutes	5
Materials needed	None
Cautions	None, **PAL = L**
Variations	None
Process questions	**Yes**

Source: Unknown

EXERCISE W - 6 · SHARK ISLAND

The purpose of this exercise is to develop trust, team work, group cohesion, and comfort with touch and movement.

The facilitator spreads several sheets of newspaper on the floor connecting the edges together to create a large enough surface that all participants can stand on it comfortably (for a group of 8 people use approximately 6-8 full sheets). The floor represents shark-infested water and the newspaper represents a safe island. When the facilitator calls "shark attack," all participants must get on the island. No part of their bodies can be touching the water. The facilitator then says it is safe to swim and everyone goes off the island. The facilitator removes one or two sheets of newspaper making a smaller island and then calls "shark attack" again. Again, when the facilitator calls shark, all participants must get on the island. No part of their bodies can be touching the water. This is repeated several times until the island is reduced to one or two sheets of newspaper requiring participants to stand using only one foot or holding some members up.

Purpose	Three Ts. Builds comfort with movement.
Level	**W**
Group size	**LG, SG**
Time ~ in minutes	5-10
Materials needed	!0-15 full sheets/pages or newspaper
Cautions	None, **PAL = M**
Variations	None
Process questions	Basic

Source: John Bergman, Geese Theatre Company

EXERCISE W - 7 · KING OR QUEEN FOR A DAY

Based on the old television show "Queen for a Day," the purpose of this exercise is to facilitate comfort with using language and words and facilitates self-disclosure.

Each group member has to tell the group what she or he would do to make the world a better place for everyone if he or she was King or Queen for a day, i.e., no one would be poor, there would be no more war.

VARIATION:

Each group member has to tell the group what she or he would do to make his or her life better if he or she could be King or Queen for a day, i.e., I would get all A's in school, my parents would stop fighting, etc.

PROCESS QUESTIONS:

Why is your idea important to you?
Does this idea reflect your values, beliefs and who you are as a person?

Purpose	Facilitates self-disclosure.
Level	**W**
Group size	**LG, SG, P, IC**
Time ~ in minutes	2-4 minutes per individual
Materials needed	None
Cautions	None, **PAL = L**
Variations	None
Process questions	**Yes**

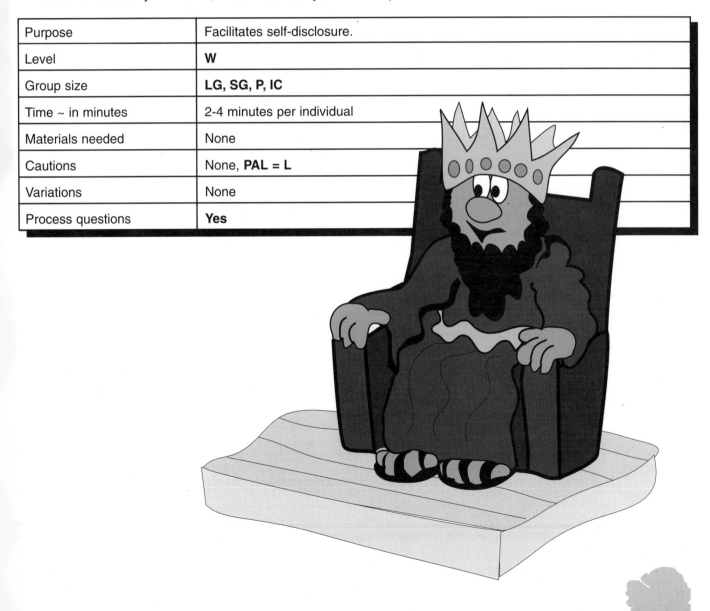

EXERCISE W - 8 · QUOTES

Quotes can be inspiring. In the book *Paths to Wellness,"* Longo, R. E. (2001) quotes are used to open and close each chapter and to accentuate various teaching points. The purpose of this exercise is to facilitate self-disclosure and to explore similarities and differences in values and beliefs between participants.

Make a list of quotes. Give the list to each person, or write them on a board or flip chart. Each person picks one quote and explains why he/she selected that particular quote. For resources on quotes, try the following web sites:

http://www.quoteland.com/index.html
http://www.quotationspage.com
http://www.bartleby.com/100

Sample list of quotes:

"We teach people what they are." ~ Pablo Casals

"I feel the capacity to care is the thing which gives life its deepest significance." ~ P. Casals

"All truth passes through three stages. First, it is ridiculed. Second, it is violently opposed. Third, it is accepted as being self evident." ~ Schopenhauer

"Children have never been very good at listening to their elders, but they have never failed to imitate them." ~ James Baldwin

"Whatever I do with a child, I will always preserve his/her dignity as a human being" ~ Haim Ginott

"Treat patients, clients, and work personnel as they 'could be' – so that they will become that:" ~ Goethe

PROCESS QUESTIONS:

Why did you select the quote?
What is similar to the way you think?
What is similar to the way you lead your life?
What feelings are you aware of when you read and think about that quote?

Purpose	Facilitate self-disclosure, and explore values and beliefs.
Level	**W**
Group size	**LG, SG, P, IC**
Time ~ in minutes	Initial exercise 5 minutes, then 3-5 minutes per participant
Materials needed	List of quotes, flip chart or dry erase board
Cautions	None, **PAL = L**
Variations	None
Process questions	**Yes**

EXERCISE W - 9 · YOU ARE WHAT YOU EAT

There is the old adage, "You are what you eat!" People also are self expressive in what they wear and what they do. The purpose of this exercise is to build trust and comfort with language and self-disclosure. It also explores similarities and differences between people.

After reading the statement, "You are what you eat!" to the group, each participant is asked to select a favorite food that represents a part of who they are as people. After each participant has selected a particular food item the group takes turns sharing what their favorite food is and why they selected it. The facilitator gives an example.

VARIATION:

Youth portray an image through the clothing they choose to wear. "You are what you wear!" Each participant takes a turn to tell a story about something they are wearing. The facilitator gives an example.

Make up a story about something you are wearing, a favorite food or favorite personal possession. The facilitator gives an example.

PROCESS QUESTIONS:

Why did you select the particular food/clothing item?
What were you thinking and feeling about your self in relationship to the selected item before you took your turn to share with the group?

Purpose	Facilitate self disclosure.
Level	**W**
Group size	**LG, SG, P, IC**
Time ~ in minutes	5-10 minutes for initial exercise and then 3-5 minutes per participant to share
Materials needed	None
Cautions	None, **PAL = L**
Variations	**Yes**
Process questions	**Yes**

EXERCISE W - 10 · ZIP, ZAP, ZOP

This exercise is a fun exercise that builds group cohesion and develops comfort with movement.

Participants stand in a circle and put their hands (palms) together. The facilitator describes three movements and the participants must pass the movement to another person in the group who then passes the same or a different movement to another group member, while saying the corresponding word that goes with the particular movement: "zip," "zap," or "zop." Participants can pass the movements on to the person next to them, across from them, or anyone in the circle.

ZIP = hands together and pass the movement to the person immediately to the left or right of him/her.
ZAP = reverses the direction of the "zip."
ZOP = throws the movement across the circle to another member.

Purpose	The purpose of this exercise is group cohesion and to develop comfort with movement.
Level	**W**
Group size	**LG, SG**
Time ~ in minutes	5-10
Materials needed	None
Cautions	None, **PAL = L**
Variations	None
Process questions	Basic

Source: John Bergman, Geese Theatre Company

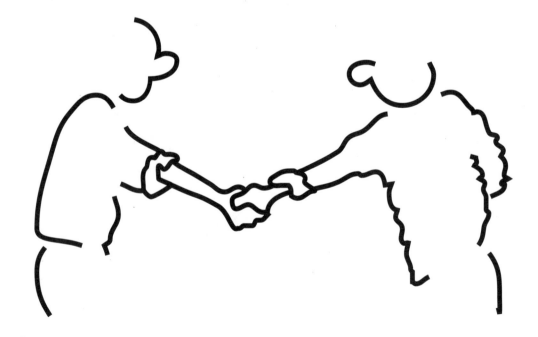

EXERCISE W - 11 · GREETING CIRCLE

The purpose of this exercise is to help participants become comfortable with language, movement, and touch.

Participants get in a circle. The facilitator selects one person to stand in the center. The facilitator goes up to the person and greets him/her in a particular way he/she chooses, i.e., hand shake, high five, hug, etc. The greeting may or may not include words, i.e. hello, how are you, what's up?, etc. The person in the center of the circle has to greet him/her back in the same way. The original person then goes and joins the circle. Another person comes to the center of the circle to greet the new participant in the center, but has to use a new and different greeting that has not been used before. The person in the center greets the person back in the same way and joins the circle. The next person comes out of the circle and greets the person in the center using a new and different greeting and the exercise is repeated until everyone has taken a turn and used a new greeting.

VARIATIONS:

Have participants form a circle. In a large room free of furniture and obstacles, the facilitator claps his hands and everyone walks into the center of the circle, back out again, and then back into the center apologizing as they do this and bump into each other.

Rude Greetings: Using the Greeting Circle or variation above, have participants do the same greeting exercise only use a "*RUDE*" greeting, i.e., a jealous look, a rude gesture (such as flipping someone the 'bird'), a rude saying, i.e., "Oh, no, not you again!," etc.

PROCESS QUESTIONS:

Begin with basic questions and then:
What was it like to be touched with a greeting?
What was it like to be greeted in a rude way (physical gesture) and/or rude verbal greeting?

Purpose	Facilitate comfort with language, movement, and touch.
Level	**W**
Group size	**LG, SG**
Time ~ in minutes	30-60 seconds per individual
Materials needed	None
Cautions	None, **PAL = M**
Variations	**Yes**
Process questions	**Yes**

Source for *Greeting Circle*: John Bergman; Geese Theatre Company

EXERCISE W - 12 · MILLING AROUND

The purpose of this exercise is to help participants become comfortable with movement and touch.

Participants mill around in the room much like in a big city or in Grand Central Station. The facilitator instructs the group that when he/she says "now" or claps his/her hands, the participants are to follow his/her instructions and that they have 7 seconds to do the task. Tasks build on each other to build comfort with touch. Examples:

Touch something red, a chair, a door.
Touch something round, a wall, and something red.
Touch something blue, a pencil, and the shoulder of two different people.
Touch a window and the elbow of another person.
Touch the arm of one person and the leg of another.
Touch the ear of one person and the nose of another person.
Touch the head of one person and the back of another person's knee at the same time.
Touch the backs of two people without letting anyone touch your back.

PROCESS QUESTIONS:

Basic and then:

How did you feel about the use of touch in this exercise?
What was most uncomfortable about the use of touch in this exercise?

Purpose	Facilitate comfort with movement and touch.
Level	**W**
Group size	**LG, SG**
Time ~ in minutes	10-15 minutes
Materials needed	Large room cleared of furniture and objects on floor
Cautions	Clear room of furniture, sharp and pointed objects, and objects on floor. Persons with physical injury or handicaps that limit movement. **PAL = H**
Variations	None
Process questions	**Yes**

Source: John Bergman; Geese Theatre Company

EXERCISE W - 13 · THE LOOK

The purpose of this exercise is to facilitate comfort with movement and look at differences between people.

Everyone mills around in a circle. When the facilitator says to model a particular "look" members continue to walk about but must use facial expressions and body gestures that capture the "look" (participants are given about 20-30 seconds per look before the next one is called). Discuss how it felt to them and how others looks affected them.

Looks:
1. "Everybody hates me." look
2. "I am better than you." look
3. "I just got all A's on my report card." look
4. "I am not valuable." look
5. "I deserve more respect." look
6. "I have too much to do." look
7. "I am jealous." look
8. "I have a cool outfit/cloths." look
9. "It's a snow day, no school!" look
10. "I like myself and I like you." look

Purpose	Facilitate comfort with movement
Level	**W**
Group size	**LG, SG**
Time ~ in minutes	5-10
Materials needed	Large room
Cautions	None, **PAL = M**
Variations	None
Process questions	Basic

Source: Adapted from Sue Forbess-Greene, L.M.S.W.

EXERCISE W - 14 · VALUES AND BELIEFS

The purpose of this exercise is to develop trust, explore movement, and differences between people.

Group participants sit in circle. Five signs are taped to the wall around the room. Signs say: Strongly Agree, Mildly Agree, Mildly Disagree, Strongly Disagree, No Opinion. The group facilitator reads statements (below) and participants go to the sign that represents their beliefs.

Statements:
1. It's okay to copy someone else's homework if they say you can do so.
2. Boys and girls are equal in all respects.
3. There is only one true religion in the world.
4. Most athletes are self-centered.
5. Bad kids come from bad families.
6. Criminals are born as criminals.
7. The press has the right to print whatever it chooses.
8. School should be year round with only a two-week summer break.
9. Every child should have his/her own phone and phone number.
10. Every family should be limited to two children.

VARIATION:

Use statements about treatment, families, or other issues.

PROCESS QUESTIONS:

What is it like (what do you think and how do you feel) when others have similar beliefs?
What is it like (what do you think and how do you feel) when others have different beliefs?

Purpose	Develop trust, explore movement, personal values and beliefs, and differences between people.
Level	**W**
Group size	**LG, SG, P, IC**
Time ~ in minutes	15-20
Materials needed	Large empty room
Cautions	None, **PAL = L**
Variations	**Yes**
Process questions	**Yes**

EXERCISE W - 15 · LINE-UPS

The purpose of this group of exercises is to help participants explore personal values and belief systems. Each exercise comes under a particular heading that describes the nature and content of the exercise. There are no "right" or "wrong" answers. Instead these exercises are designed to help participants explore their values and beliefs and see how they differ from other participants.

These exercises involve participants in simple fun without verbal communication or signaling (no talking signaling is important). Looking at each other they are to put themselves in a line according to what they perceive is their position as compared to others based upon the nature of the exercise. The facilitator tells participants which end of the line is for one area or extreme and which is for the other area or extreme, i.e., the left end of the line is the tallest person and the right end is the shortest person.

Height: Without talking or any communication participants are asked to get in a line in order of their height, the tallest on one end of the line the shortest participant on the opposite end of the line.

VARIATIONS:

Birthday: Without talking or any communication participants are asked to get in a line in order of their birthday. Then starting at the youngest person's end, each person states his or her age and birth date to see how close they came to being right.

Similarities and Differences: Participants stand in a straight line side by side. The right side of the line is agree (similar beliefs) the left side is disagree (differing beliefs). The facilitator them gives the participants statements to which they agree or disagree or have similarities or differences. Examples for line-ups:

EVERYONE WHO:
Likes to shop.
Likes to baby sit.
Likes to go out for dinner.
Like to drive fast.

Likes and Dislikes: Participants sit in a circle with paper and pencil. Each writes down three characteristics about him/herself that he/she most likes and then writes down three characteristics about him/herself he/she most dislikes. After everyone is done each member shares their list with the group. After each person shares, the group discusses briefly their perceptions of that person.

VARIATION: Participants stand up and an imaginary line is drawn. One end is "likes this a lot" and the other end is "does not like this at all." Participants are asked to put themselves somewhere in the line based upon their personal likes and dislikes after each of the following statements is read by the facilitator. Likes and dislikes should be used that will create differences and extremes between participants. For example, most people like pizza (little extreme), while many people do not like to baby sit (will generally create extremes. The facilitator reads one of the following examples/statements below (or make up a list of your own) at a time to participants. Everyone who likes to:

'Go shopping."
'Go out to dinner."
'Baby sit."
'House cleaning."
'Do laundry."
'Go out with people you have just met." (Or never met before).

Similarities: Participants stand up in a circle and the facilitator tells them to form groups of similarities, i.e., eye color (brown, blue, hazel, etc.) shoe size, brand of car they like, favorite foods.

Purpose	To explore personal values and beliefs.
Level	**W**
Group size	**LG, SG**
Time ~ in minutes	5 per exercise
Materials needed	None
Cautions	None, **PAL. = M**
Variations	**Yes**
Process questions	Basic

EXERCISE W - 16 · BODY EXPRESSION

The purpose of this exercise is to facilitate movement and comfort with self expression.

The group stands in a circle. The facilitator explains the goal of this exercise is to use different body parts to express certain emotions. Each participant is given a slip of paper upon which there is a body part and an emotion. Participants do not share with each other. One by one, each group member has to guess what emotion is being portrayed as the person in center acts out the emotion with that body part. Discussion ensues about non-verbal expression of feelings and emotions.

Love - feet

Boredom – legs

Fear - mouth

Excitement - mouth

Sorrow - shoulders

Exhaustion – waist

Reverence - arms

Impatience - feet

Anger – hands

Tenderness - hands

Surprise - hands

Loathing - arms

Hate – fingers

Terror – mouth

Frustration - eyes

Exasperation - eyes

Disgust - arms

Puzzlement - shoulders

Sadness - mouth

Joyfulness - fingers

PROCESS QUESTIONS:

What was fun about this exercise?

What was difficult about this exercise?

Did you feel silly or self-conscious? Why?

Purpose	To facilitate movement and comfort with self-expression.
Level	**W**
Group size	**LG, SG**
Time ~ in minutes	3-5 minutes per participant
Materials needed	Large open space
Cautions	None, **PAL = M**
Variations	None
Process questions	**Yes**

Source: Adapted from Sue Forbess-Greene, L.M.S.W.

EXERCISE W - 17 · "ZACK"

The purpose of this exercise is to facilitate trust and team building.

Take a small stuffed animal that fits in your pocket. Name it 'Zack' or whatever name you like. 'Zack' is used as a tool to facilitate everyone getting to know each others' names and setting a goal for the day or sharing something about one's self. The object of 'Zack' is to serve as an ice-breaker.

The facilitator pulls out 'Zack' and says, " Hi 'Zack' my name is ___and today I hope to... (set a goal or personal dis closure).

The facilitator passes it on to the person to his/her left. That person says, "Hello 'Zack' My name is Jill and to my right is Jack. Today I hope to... Then 'Zack' is passed on to that person's left. The next person says hello 'Zack' my name is Joe and this is Jill and Jack. Today I hope to.... And, so it goes until everyone has had a turn.

PROCESS QUESTIONS:

What was fun about this exercise?
What was hard?
Did you feel embarrassed? Why?

Purpose	To facilitate trust and team building.
Level	**W**
Group size	**LG, SG**
Time ~ in minutes	20-30 minutes
Materials needed	Small pocket sized stuffed toy/animal
Cautions	None, **PAL = L**
Variations	None
Process questions	**Yes**

Source: Mark Bartleson

EXERCISE W - 18 · PEEK A BOO

The purpose of this exercise is to facilitate team building.

Divide people into two teams. Then hold up a sheet. Each team squats behind the sheet so that no one can see the members of the other team. One person on each team gets up in front next to the sheet. When the sheet is dropped the first team member to identify the person in front on the other team/side wins and that person comes over to the other side and joins the opposite team. Repeat the exercise and continue until one team is eliminated.

Purpose	Facilitate team building.
Level	**W**
Group size	**LG, SG**
Time ~ in minutes	10-15 minutes
Materials needed	Large piece of cloth, canvas, or sheet
Cautions	None, **PAL = M**
Variations	None
Process questions	Basic

Source: Mark Bartleson

EXERCISE W - 19 · LOOKING FOR 'ZOË'

The purpose of this exercise is to facilitate trust.

Participants get into a circle and close their eyes. One participant is identified by the facilitator as 'Zoë'. Zoë can open his eyes but cannot talk or make any noise. The others must keep their eyes closed but can talk. Everyone is free to move about in the room or area including Zoë. The task is for each participant to find Zoë (Hint: remember Zoë can NOT talk or make any sounds). Once a participant finds Zoë, he/she holds onto Zoë's arm and can open his/her eyes but cannot talk or make any sounds. All participants move around looking for Zoë until everyone finds him/her.

PROCESS QUESTIONS:

How did it feel to walk around blinded alone?
How did it feel to walk around with others holding onto you?

Purpose	Three Ts.
Level	**W**
Group size	**LG, SG**
Time ~ in minutes	10-15 minutes
Materials needed	Large room or space to work in
Cautions	Make sure room/area is free of objects to trip over or bump into, **PAL = L**
Variations	None
Process questions	**Yes**

Source: Mark Bartleson

EXERCISE W - 20 · BRIDGE

The purpose of this exercise is to build trust.

Participants pair off with someone close to their height and weight. The two people face each other and put their palms to the palms of the other person. Keeping their backs straight and legs slightly spread apart each moves backwards (Keeping their palms together) as they form a human bridge. How far can they go?

PROCESS QUESTIONS:

Were you afraid to do the exercise? If so, why?
What was hardest about forming the bridge?

Purpose	Facilitate trust building.
Level	**W**
Group size	**LG, SG, P**
Time ~ in minutes	2-3 minutes per pair
Materials needed	None
Cautions	**Yes**. Physical safety. **PAL = H**
Variations	None
Process questions	**Yes**

Source: Mark Bartleson

EXERCISE W - 21 · FALLING

The purpose of this exercise is to facilitate trust and team building.

Participants pair off with someone of a similar height and weight. Each person practices taking a karate stance, holding hands out and flattening thumbs by the side of each hand (this protects the thumbs). One participant then turns standing with his/her back to the other person, about 1 foot away. The person with his/her back to the other now closes his/her eyes and falls back toward the other person's hands whose task it is to hold that person up. your hands. Repeat at 2 feet repeat at 30 inches, etc.

VARIATIONS:

Metronome: Two participants pair off as above with hands out. A third person gets in the middle facing away from both. The person in the middle falls to one side and that person stops him/her and gently pushes the person up and over to the other person forming a human Metronome. The pair pushes the person side to side.

Falling Circle: All participants stand in a circle with one participant in the center of the circle. The person in the center closes his/her eyes. He/she must keep feet together and stand in very center of circle. Everyone in the circle puts their hands out and slowly and gently passes the person in the center around the circle, as that person keeps his/her feet firmly planted to the ground in the circle's center. Once the group is working together they can pass the person in the center around more quickly, switching directions a few times. Don't let him/her fall.

PROCESS QUESTIONS:

Were you afraid to do the exercise?
If so, why?
What was hardest about falling?
Was it easy or hard to trust others?

Purpose	Facilitate trust and team building.
Level	**W**
Group size	**LG, SG**
Time ~ in minutes	5-10 minutes
Materials needed	Large open area free of objects on the ground or objects to bump into.
Cautions	None. **PAL= H**
Variations	**Yes**
Process questions	**Yes**

Source: Mark Bartleson

EXERCISE W - 22 · LUNAR EMERGENCY

The purpose of this exercise is to facilitate team work.

Use cord or rope to make a 10 foot square on the ground. All participants stand in the square. Pull out the box of 2x4 strips of wood (wood strips should be 8-14 inches long). If there are 12 people in square, pull out 11 pieces of wood, one less than number of people in the square. About thirty to forty feet away are three hula hoops stacked on the ground. The square is a lunar space station and the hoops are rocket ships back to earth that only hold up to 4 people each.

The goal of the exercise is that the team must get from the lunar station to the rocket ships before the station is destroyed by a meteorite. They can do this only as a team by using the oxygen blocks (2x4 wood strips) to move between the station and the rocket ships. All team members must maintain contact. If anyone falls off an oxygen block they can be awarded a handicap by the facilitator, i.e., one broken arm, etc. Once 4 people get in the hoops, they can lift one hoop over their heads and lay it on the ground allowing 4 more to be in a space ship, as long as the hoops are always touching.

PROCESS QUESTIONS:

What was it like to work as a team?
Did a facilitator emerge?

Purpose	Facilitate team work.
Level	**W, I**
Group size	**LG**, 10-15
Time ~ in minutes	30
Materials needed	Blocks of wood 2x4 and several each between 8-14 inches long. Three or four hula-hoops. 40 feet of cord or rope.
Cautions	Clear area of any objects that are sharp, **PAL = M**
Variations	None
Process questions	**Yes**

Source: Mark Bartleson

EXERCISE W - 23 · POINTS OF CONTACT

The purpose of this exercise is to facilitate, trust, teamwork, and comfort with touch.

The facilitator divides the participants into small groups of 4 - 6 people. Participants are instructed that each person has 5 points of contact, 2 feet, two hands, and their buttocks. Points of contact are the only body parts allowed to make contact with the floor.

The small groups have to maintain physical contact with each other i.e. holding hands locking arms etc. The facilitator starts the exercise by telling the groups to establish 15 points of contact , i.e. with 6 people per group, each participant has both feet on the floor and three people touch one hand to the floor (total 15 points of contact, while maintaining contact with each other). The facilitator then begins to reduce the number of points of contact to the lowest point the groups can go, 13, 11, then 9, 7, then 5, 3, etc. They can lift themselves off the ground or they can use chairs, but don't give the groups any hints... let the participants figure out creative ways to establish the points of contact. The facilitator may see such creative process such as hopping on each others backs, picking each other up, building a pyramid, etc.

Purpose	The Three Ts
Level	**W**
Group size	**LG, SG**
Time ~ in minutes	5 -10
Materials needed	None
Cautions	None. **PAL = H**
Variations	None
Process questions	Basic

Source: John Bergman, Geese Theatre Company

EXERCISE W - 24 · HUMAN KNOT

The purpose of this old and popular exercise is to facilitate, trust, teamwork, and comfort with touch.

Have the participants form a circle, and stick their left hand out into the circle. Then each person reaches across with their right hand and grabs the left hand of another. This forms a human knot. The group is instructed to get the knot untangled and form a circle without letting go.

VARIATION:

Same as above, only if the group is not able to undo the knot and form a circle, they can make one magic change.

PROCESS QUESTIONS:

Identify who were the leaders. How does it feel doing the exercise?
Did you experience discomfort when having close contact with others?

Purpose	The Three Ts
Level	**W**
Group size	**LG, SG**
Time ~ in minutes	5 -10
Materials needed	None.
Cautions	None. **PAL = H**
Variations	**Yes**
Process questions	**Yes**

Source: Unknown

EXERCISE W - 25 · SWAPPING STORIES

The purpose of this exercise is to facilitate self-disclosure and help participants feel more comfortable and accepted in the group, especially when they are newcomers.

Participants pair up in twos and swap stories. The facilitator can ask them to swap stories about a variety of things such as: something bad they did (i.e., an offense), a happy occasion, a time they felt sad, their greatest accomplishment, the worst experience in their life, etc. They are expected share with as much detail as possible including feelings. The dyad then presents each other's story to the rest of the group.

PROCESS QUESTIONS:

What was easiest to disclose to others?
What was hardest to disclose to others?
Did you hold back from sharing?

Purpose	To facilitate self disclosure and help participants feel more comfortable and accepted in the group
Level	**W**
Group size	**LG, SG, P**
Time ~ in minutes	20 - 30
Materials needed	None
Cautions	None. **PAL = L**
Variations	None
Process questions	**Yes**

Source: Susan Robinson: Growing Beyond. NEARI Press.

EXERCISE W, I - 26 · TRUST FALL

The purpose of this exercise is to facilitate trust and team building.

A sturdy solid object that a person can stand on (table, wooden platform or deck) is used in the center of the room or area. 4-5 participants form two lines facing each other extending out from the table or platform. With each line facing each other they stand shoulder to shoulder and extend their arms out alternating arms with the person across from them forming what looks like a "zipper" pattern with arms. One person stands at the end of the line facing both lines and the table or deck with his/her arms extended (this serves to protect the falling person's head). The arms of each participant should be touching the arms of the others to form a tight "zipper."

One participant at a time gets on the table/deck, turns his/her back to the human zipper, closes his/her eyes and falls backwards (keeping body as straight and rigid as possible) into their arms (zipper). As each participant takes a turn others fill in to form the human zipper.

PROCESS QUESTIONS:

Were you afraid to do the exercise?
If so, why?
What was hardest about falling?

Purpose	Facilitate trust and team building.
Level	**W, I**
Group size	**LG, SG**
Time ~ in minutes	3-5 minutes per participant
Materials needed	Table or tall safe object to stand on that is 3-4 feet tall
Cautions	Use safeguards to prevent injury, remove glasses, objects from body, etc. **PAL = H**
Variations	None
Process questions	**Yes**

Source: Unknown

EXERCISE W, I - 27 · INTRODUCE YOUR PARTNER

The purpose of this exercise is to help participants build trust in others and comfort with using words and expressing feelings. This exercise also helps facilitate self disclosure, personal sharing, and developing relationships.

Participants pair off with someone they don't know well. Each pair has to find out three pieces of information about the person he/she has paired off with, the person's name (or weight) and two additional facts about the person. Each participant takes a turn reporting to the group what they learned about the person he/she paired off with.

VARIATIONS:

Personal Story: Participants pair off and share a personal story with each other that they have not told many other people.

Variation: Participants take turns sharing their partner's story with the rest of the group.

PROCESS QUESTIONS:

Did you feel comfortable sharing? Why?
Did you share something new you have not told another?
Did you withhold sharing certain aspects of your life story?

Purpose	Facilitate self disclosure, trust building.
Level	**W, I**
Group size	**P**
Time ~ in minutes	10-15
Materials needed	None
Cautions	None, **PAL = L**
Variations	**Yes**
Process questions	**Yes**

Source: Unknown

EXERCISE W, 1 - 28 · MEDIA EXPERT

The purpose of this exercise is to facilitate comfort with using language and words and facilitate self- disclosure.

The facilitator picks four participants. One is selected as the "expert" and the others are interviewers from the media. The facilitator assigns a topic to the "expert" and the media interviewers take turns asking him/her 3 or 4 questions. Then the "expert" becomes an interviewer and a new "expert" is selected and is now the expert of a new topic.

VARIATION:

As the experts change, a new topic is selected that ups the anti, and the affect.

Examples of expert topics:
"American trouser fleas"
"Invisible dental floss"
"Soleless shoes"

More intense topics:
"Standing on your head to manage anger"
"Bubble gum as contraceptive device"

Most intense topics:
"Impact of sexual abuse of victims"
"Handling death of a friend"
"Lose of a parent"
"Incest"

PROCESS QUESTIONS:

As the topics became more serious was it harder to ask questions or answer them?
Did some of the topics make you feel uncomfortable? If so, why?

Purpose	Facilitate self-disclosure.
Level	**W, I**
Group size	**SG -4, P, IC**
Time ~ in minutes	5- 10 minutes per group
Materials needed	None
Cautions	**Yes**, can trigger issues that need therapeutic follow-up/attention. **PAL = L**
Variations	**Yes**
Process questions	**Yes**

Source: John Bergman, Geese Theatre Company

EXERCISE W, 1 - 29 · THROUGH THE DOOR

This exercise builds individual confidence and enhances comfort with movement and words.

Each participant takes a turn walking through a door (or an imaginary door if there is not a door to the room). Each person must enter the doorway in a different fashion than the previous participants. Entering through the door can be silent or with the use of words or phrases generated by the participant.

VARIATION:

The facilitator can instruct the participants who/what lies in waiting on the other side of the door. Examples include:

1. The door goes to an unknown room/place.
2. When you enter the room there is a good friend you have not seen in years.
3. When you enter the room there is a stranger.
4. When you enter the room there is one or both of your parents.
5. When you enter the room there is a person whom has hurt you in the past.
6. When you enter the room there is a person you do not like or trust.

PROCESS QUESTIONS:

Why did you choose the scenario behind the door you mimed?
Was there a door you thought about going through but decided not to?

Purpose	Enhance comfort with movement and words.
Level	**W, I**
Group size	**LG, SG,** one at a time, **P, IC**
Time ~ in minutes	30-60 seconds per person
Materials needed	Doorway, or imaginary doorway
Cautions	None, **PAL = M**
Variations	**Yes**
Process questions	**Yes**

Source: John Bergman; Geese Theatre Company

EXERCISE W, I - 30 · I'M LIKE A . . .

When our kids were young we played a game in the car called "I'm Thinking of an Animal" and while one person thought of an animal, the rest of us had to try to guess what animal the person was thinking about. The purpose of this exercise is to facilitate self-disclosure and explore similarities and differences in values and beliefs between participants.

Each participant is asked to select a particular animal, i.e., lion, frog, worm, giraffe, dog, mouse, alligator, etc. that represents most closely who they are and then share why they selected that particular animal with the group, by saying, I'm most like a ___ because...

VARIATIONS:

Pair off and share with a partner or work in groups of three or four.

Instead of "life" situations use specific situations such as being in treatment, situations in the community, being with peers/friends, living at home, situations in school, etc.

Use traffic signals and road signs. Each participant selects a particular traffic signal (i.e., stop light, walk sign, caution light, etc.) or road sign, (i.e., stop sign, information sign, caution sign, speed sign, etc.), and takes a few minutes to write down what "life" situations correlate to the traffic signal of road sign he/she has selected. "I'm most like a _____ because...

Use various shapes, i.e., box, circle, diamond, octagon, oval, etc. Then each person says I'm most like a _____ because....

Have participants select their favorite vehicle, plane, boat, train, bus, car, truck and particular model or type, i.e., Ford Mustang, speed boat, jet, steam engine, etc. Then each person says I'm most like a _____ because....

PROCESS QUESTIONS:

Why did you select the particular animal/sign/shape/vehicle?
What was easy about sharing with others?
What was hard about sharing with others?
What are the most important life issues you believe you are faced with?
What similarities did you discover between yourself and others in the group?

Purpose	Facilitate self-disclosure.
Level	**W, I**
Group size	**LG, SG, P, IC**
Time ~ in minutes	5-10 minutes per participant
Materials needed	None
Cautions	None, **PAL = L**
Variations	**Yes**
Process questions	**Yes**

EXERCISE W, 1 - 31 · EXPLORING ENVIRONMENTS

The purpose of this exercise is to facilitate comfort with movement and self-exploration.

Participants stand up in a large open space and begin walking around. The facilitator describes one at a time different environments in a sequence and the participants begin to walk around as if they are in the environment described. The facilitator uses a hand clap to announce an environment change will be next. Allow ample time, 30-60 seconds, for participants to experience each environment before clapping and changing environments.

Sample environment sequence:

It is chilly outside...
Now it is warm...
There is a small breeze...
The breeze gets cooler...
It begins to rain...
It is night now...

You can continue to use this sequence and make up new ones or create new lists of environments.

VARIATION:

You come across a mine field...
There is a box in the ground...
You take the box ...
You look in the box...
You see a hedge...
Behind the hedge is a house...
You go into the house...
You see a large TV screen...
There is a movie on the TV...
The movie is about you...

Allow ample time, 30-60 seconds, for participants to experience each environment before clapping and changing environments. You will want to allow more time to explore the box and to watch the movie.

PROCESS QUESTIONS:

How did it feel to change environments?
Were any one of the environments hard to be in?
What was in the box?
What was the movie about?

Purpose	Facilitate comfort with movement and self-exploration.
Level	**W, I**
Group size	**LG, SG**
Time ~ in minutes	5-10; Variation 10-20
Materials needed	Large room
Cautions	The more intense variation can open up issues. **PAL = H**
Variations	**Yes**
Process questions	**Yes**

Source: John Bergman, Geese Theatre Company

EXERCISE W, 1 - 32 · WORDS & PHRASES

The purpose of this exercise is to develop comfort with the use of words and language and facilitate handling disagreement.

Participants stand in a circle. The facilitator selects two participants to stand in the center of the circle. The two participants are given one word each and they take turns one at a time saying to each other the word they were assigned. The two words are, "yes" and "no." Repeat the exercise until all participants have done the exercise. Participants are paired off and assigned person "A" and person "B." After pairing off, person "A" is assigned the word *yes* and person "B" is assigned the word *no*. Maintaining eye contact is important.

VARIATIONS:

The group pairs off and pairs do the exercise simultaneously.

Four Words: Participants stand in a circle. The facilitator selects two participants to stand in the center of the circle and have a conversation. The two participants are instructed they can only use the four words given by the facilitator, i.e., fish, dumb, go, taxi OR tree, come, chair, frog. Repeat until all participants have done the exercise.

Variation of Four Words: Up the ante… use four words that have more affect and more power, i.e., weak, victim, fear, stay

Two Phrases: Participants stand in a circle. The facilitator selects two participants to stand in the center of the circle. The two participants are given one of two phrases that are oppositional and they take turns one at a time saying to each other the assigned phrase. Select two more participants and assign them the same or a new phrase. Successive pairs continue to do the exercise until everyone has had a turn. Examples of phrases include:

"I can do it myself" and "I will do it for you"
"I want to talk now" and "I need time to think"
"Please don't tell"   and "I must tell him/her now"
"I want you to stay" and "I really need to go"
"I need it now" and "You can have it later"

PROCESS QUESTIONS:

What did you feel during the exercise?
Was your verbal behavior passive, assertive or aggressive?
When you switched roles was the feeling any different?

Purpose	To develop comfort with the use of words and language and facilitate handling disagreement.
Level	**W, I**
Group size	**LG, SG, P, IC**
Time ~ in minutes	2-3 per pair, per exercise
Materials needed	None
Cautions	None, **PAL = L**
Variations	**Yes**
Process questions	**Yes**

Source: John Bergman, Geese Theatre Company

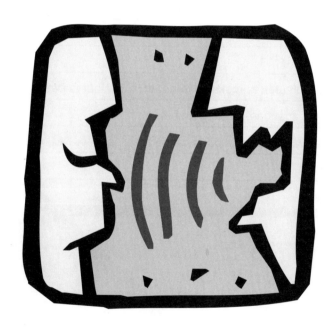

EXERCISE W, I - 33 · MY LIFE DRAWING

The purpose of this exercise is to facilitate self-disclosure.

The facilitator gives each participant a sheet of paper and access to crayons, pens, markers, etc. Each participant draws a picture that represents "*My Life*" and puts his/her name on it. Drawings are collected, and redistributed randomly. (If a participant gets his/her own drawing back, swap it with another participant.) Each participant then introduces the person whose drawing he/she has and tells that person's story by interpreting the drawing. The artist may not interrupt the person while they are talking. After each person in the group is done, the artist can then make any corrections about the story and misconceptions.

VARIATION:

Give the group a particular topic to use for drawing the picture, i.e., family, being in treatment, my personal problems, when I was abused, etc.

PROCESS QUESTIONS:

Did you draw a "safe" drawing or one that was revealing?
How did it feel when another saw your drawing and understood what it meant?
How did it feel when another saw your drawing and misinterpreted it?

Purpose	Facilitate self-disclosure
Level	**W, I**
Group size	**LG, SG, P, IC**
Time ~ in minutes	5-10 minutes to make drawing, then 5 minutes per participant
Materials needed	Paper, crayons, pens, markers
Cautions	**Yes**. Variations can open up personal issues. **PAL = L**
Variations	**Yes**
Process questions	**Yes**

Source: Adapted from Sue Forbess-Greene, L.M.S.W.

EXERCISE W, I - 34 · THINGS THAT ARE

The purpose of this exercise is to facilitate self-disclosure.

The facilitator has a list of words and explains to the group that some things just are!! The facilitator explains that he/she will give a category and the participants will respond with an answer. ("One person's positive experience is another's nightmare.") So if facilitator says "Things that are *Hard*...." then each participant will write down and then share how they responded to the question.

Sample statements:

Things that are *hard*
Things that are *easy*
Things that are *scary*
Things that are *funny*
Things that are *unusual*
Things that are *boring*
Things that are *exciting*

VARIATIONS:

Use the same basic exercise above but use one of the following statements:

Things that are hard/easy/etc. about *Treatment*
Things that are hard/easy/etc. about *Living at home*
Things that are hard/easy/etc. about *School*
Things that are hard/easy/etc. about *Having friends*
Things that are hard/easy/etc. about *Having no friends*
Things that are hard/easy/etc. about *Not living at home*

PROCESS QUESTIONS:

What does it feel like to have similar thoughts and views as others?
What does it feel like to have different thoughts and feelings about others?
What was hardest to share?

Purpose	To facilitate self-disclosure
Level	**W, I**
Group size	**LG, SG, P, IC**
Time ~ in minutes	For a group of 12, each statement takes about 15-20 minutes
Materials needed	Pencil, paper
Cautions	**Yes**. Can open up personal issues, **PAL = L**
Variations	**Yes**
Process questions	**Yes**

Source: Adapted from Sue Forbess-Greene, L.M.S.W.

EXERCISE W, I - 35 · IN THE HOT SEAT

One of the oldest Gestalt Therapy techniques is called the "Hot Seat." This exercise is a spin off of that particular technique. The purpose of this exercise is to facilitate communication, discussion, and personal sharing.

The group sits in a circle and one chair (Hot Seat) is put in the center of the circle. The facilitator asks the group to make a list of qualifications they think are important to be a "good therapist" on a sheet of paper. Group discussion follows as each person takes a turn sitting in the "Hot Seat" and reading from his/her list. Other topics might include:

- Being a good child-care worker/social worker.
- Being a good parent.
- Being a good school teacher.
- Being a good son/daughter.

VARIATION:

Exercise is done with each patient one by one and topics range about personal issues/ problems, self-improvement, and/or treatment related issues.

Repeat the initial exercise with a new/different topic.

PROCESS QUESTIONS:

What experiences have you had with therapists, social workers, parents, teachers, etc. that influenced your comments/discussion?
What could therapists, social workers, and others do to improve what they do?
What could therapists, social workers, and others do to improve their relationship with you?

Purpose	To facilitate communication, discussion, and personal sharing.
Level	**W, I**
Group size	**LG, SG, P, IC**
Time ~ in minutes	20-30 minutes per exercise/topic
Materials needed	One chair
Cautions	**Yes**. May open up personal issues, **PAL = L**
Variations	**Yes**
Process questions	**Yes**

EXERCISE W, I - 36 · MUSICAL SECRETS

This exercise is based upon one of the older and more popular children's games musical chairs. The purpose of this exercise is to facilitate communication, discussion, and personal sharing.

The facilitator has everyone sit in a chair in a circle. One person is selected to stand up and his/her chair is removed from the circle. Everyone stands up and music is played as people walk around the outside of the circle of chairs. When the music stops, everyone tries to sit in a chair and one person will remain standing, as there is one chair short. The person left standing goes to the center of the circle and tells a personal secret about him/her self.

Afterward, that person sits in a chair and everyone else stands up and the music starts. The person who has told a secret remains seated the rest of the time while others stand and walk around the chair circle during the music. The process is repeated over and over until everyone in the group has had the opportunity to share a personal secret.

VARIATION:

Using the same exercise above, each client has to take a turn sharing something personal. Make up categories or use the ones below.

• Something they *like* about themselves (personal strengths).
• Something they *dislike* about themselves (personal weaknesses).
• A lie they told that got them into trouble.
• The most embarrassing moment in their life.
• The worst thing they did that got them into serious trouble.

PROCESS QUESTIONS:

What was easiest about this exercise? Why?
What was hard about this exercise? Why?
What does it feel like to be honest?
What does it feel like to lie?
Where there things you thought about telling the group and decided not to?

Purpose	To facilitate communication, discussion, and personal sharing.
Level	**W, I**
Group size	**LG, SG**
Time ~ in minutes	2-5 minutes per person.
Materials needed	Large room and chairs
Cautions	**Yes**. May open up personal issues, **PAL = L**
Variations	**Yes**
Process questions	**Yes**

CHAPTER FOUR — INTRODUCTORY LEVEL EXERCISES

EXERCISE I - 1 · FLASH-CARD PAPER WALK

The purpose of this exercise is to facilitate self-disclosure and exploration of problematic behavior.

One or more group members identify a problem behavior they want to explore or the therapist has indicated the person needs to explore. The participant describes the behavior or incident and the facilitator makes stepping-stones from the sheets of paper to form a walk-way or path. Each sheet has a link (thought, feeling, or behavior) in the chain of behaviors that led up to the problematic behavior or incident. The flash card set (Appendix C), may also be used in lieu of or in conjunction with custom made stepping stone sheets.

The steps are put down in order forming a path that leads to the problem behavior. As the participant moves along the path the facilitator or other participants help the individual explore interventions, coping responses or behavioral options to move off the path to ruin. Paper steps with arrows pointing to alternatives and choices are set down at key steps on the path and the participant explores options, correctives, coping responses. This is a good exercise to use with lower functioning and/or learning disabled patients.

PROCESS QUESTIONS:

What did you learn about your behavior/problem?
Did you learn alternative ways of behaving or coping?
What was easiest to do? What was most difficult to do?
What was most embarrassing?

Purpose	Facilitate self-disclosure and exploration of problematic behavior.
Level	**I**
Group size	**LG, SG, P, IC**
Time ~ in minutes	20-30
Materials needed	Open space, sheets of paper, magic markers
Cautions	**Yes**. Can open up thoughts and feelings, **PAL = L**
Variations	None
Process questions	**Yes**

Source: Matthew Doyle, New Hope Treatment Centers

EXERCISE 1 - 2 · ROAD MAP

The purpose of this exercise is to facilitate self-exploration and self-disclosure.

Each participant is given a large sheet (3-4 feet long) of rolled newspaper print paper or a sheet of paper from a flip chart. A variety of pens, pencils, markers, crayons, etc. are provided to the group. Each participant makes a 'Road Map' of his/her life on the paper. The map begins with his/her past life, then proceeds to his/her present life, and ends with his/her future life (where the participant sees him/her self in the future.

PROCESS QUESTIONS:

How do you see yourself changing in the future?
What are the road blocks and obstacles?
What will be the hardest task to accomplish?

Purpose	Facilitate self-exploration and self-disclosure.
Level	I
Group size	**LG, SG, P, IC**
Time ~ in minutes	10-15
Materials needed	Large roll or sheets of paper, pencils, pens, markers, crayons
Cautions	**Yes**. Can open up personal issues, **PAL = L**
Variations	None
Process questions	**Yes**

EXERCISE 1 - 3 · WHO AM I? COLLAGE

Purpose of exercise is to facilitate self-exploration and self-disclosure.

Each participant is given a large sheet (6-7 foot long) of rolled newspaper print paper (or tape two sheets from a flip chart together end to end). A variety of pens, pencils, markers, crayons, etc and magazines are provided to the group. Each participant lays down on the paper and another participant makes an outline of the participants body on the paper (use pencil to avoid damage to clothing). When everyone has an outline of their body each participant then begins to make a collage of him/her self and life. Participants can use words and or phrases, color or draw, and/or glue down pictures on the outline of their body.

VARIATION:

Three Dimensional Collage (Source: Cindy Tyo, New Hope Treatment Centers)

The purpose of this exercise is to facilitate expression of both the outer and inner self with a sense of security.

The individual is given a large envelop, scissors, markers, glue and magazines and is instructed to create a collage of his/her self using both the outside and the inside of the envelope. The outside is to represent what other's see and know about the individual. The inside represents what other's do not see or know about the individual. The inner contributions should not be glued inside the envelope as the individual may choose to bring them to the outside.

Once the collage is completed, the therapist encourages the individual to begin to share the objects on the outside of the envelope working toward sharing the inside.

PROCESS QUESTIONS:

Explain your collage addressing the thoughts and feelings you had when making it.
How did it feel to explore your future?

Purpose	Facilitate self-disclosure.
Level	**I**
Group size	**LG, SG, P, IC**
Time ~ in minutes	20-30
Materials needed	Large roll or sheets of paper, pencils, pens, markers, crayons. A variety of magazines etc. with pictures.
Cautions	**Yes**. Can open up personal issues, **PAL = L**
Variations	**Yes**
Process questions	**Yes**

EXERCISE 1 - 4 · TIME CAPSULE

The purpose of this exercise is to facilitate self-disclosure and personal sharing.

The day before this exercise the facilitator gives all participants a copy of the *Time Capsule Worksheet* (Appendix C). Send out time capsule activity sheet to everyone. Organize people into groups of 4-6. Each table has a box with a lid on it that represents a time capsule. Ask people to put their treasures into the time capsule. Each group takes turns opening up the time capsule and selects one item. The owner of the item taken from the box explains the item to the group.

PROCESS QUESTIONS:

Why did you choose the items you selected for the time capsule?
Which item has the most meaning and why?
Was any item hard to share? Why?
What thoughts were you aware of as you did this exercise and shared?
What feelings were you aware of as you did this exercise and shared?

Purpose	Facilitate self-disclosure and personal sharing.
Level	**I**
Group size	**LG, SG**
Time ~ in minutes	5-10 minutes per person
Materials needed	Time capsule work sheet, box
Cautions	**Yes**. Can open up issues. **PAL = L**
Variations	None
Process questions	**Yes**

Source: Adapted from Sue Forbess-Greene, L.M.S.W.

EXERCISE 1 - 5 · FREE ASSOCIATIONS

The purpose of this exercise is to facilitate self-disclosure and self-exploration.

The facilitator can work with the entire group or have participants count off by threes and then divide the group into groups of three. The facilitator prepares a list or words or phrases in advance. Before the exercise the facilitator gives participants the list of words or writes them on a flip chart or board. Each person has a few minutes to write down one or two associations to each word. Each person then shares with the group their associations with each word. The associations can be single words, phrases, or sentences.

Sample word list: childbirth, graduation, chocolate, patriotism, family, school, love, hate, parents, brother, sister.

VARIATIONS:

Instead of a list of words, put up pictures for participants to see.

Wordy Connections (Cindy Tyo, New Hope Treatment Centers)

The purpose of this exercise is also to facilitate self-disclosure and self-exploration.

The facilitator makes up a list of ten words. Each participant makes 3 columns on a sheet of paper numbered 1-10 with headings "First Thought" (word) "First Feelings" "First Action" (word). The facilitator reads one word at a time. Participants are instructed to write down the first thought/word that comes to mind after the word is read aloud, and write it in the first column. Repeat and write down the first feeling, repeat and write down the first action. Everyone then shares their response with the group. Examples of words: family, holidays, friends, lying, violence, anger, school, work, treatment, abuse, etc.

PROCESS QUESTIONS:

Which word created the most memories for you?
What was the memory?
What thoughts came to mind?
Which word created the more intense feelings for you?
What feelings did you experience?

Purpose	Facilitate self-disclosure and self exploration.
Level	**I**
Group size	**LG, SG, P, IC**
Time ~ in minutes	1-2 minutes per word, 10-15 minutes per word category
Materials needed	Word list or pictures, paper and pencil
Cautions	**Yes**. May open up personal issues. **PAL = L**
Variations	**Yes**
Process questions	**Yes** (Discussion after each word association is optional.)

EXERCISE 1 - 6 · GETTING TO KNOW YOU

The purpose of this exercise is to facilitate self-disclosure, risk taking.

The facilitator has the participants sit in a circle with one chair in the middle. Each participant has a pencil and sheets of paper. One person sits in the middle and each group member writes three adjectives down that describe the person, first impressions, etc., (if this is a first time meeting with participants they take turns spending 3-5 minutes each telling the other participants something about him/her self). The sheets of paper are collected and given to the participant in the chair in the center of the circle, but he/she cannot read them. Each participant does this. When everyone is done, then each participant writes down three adjectives about him/herself. Each person then takes a turn to read the adjectives written about him or herself to the group, and then reads his or her own adjectives after reading out loud how others described him or her.

PROCESS QUESTIONS:

Were your self-descriptions different than how others saw you?
What do you think/feel about the similarities and differences of how others perceive you?

Purpose	Facilitate self-disclosure.
Level	**I**
Group size	**LG, SG, P**
Time ~ in minutes	5-10 minutes per person
Materials needed	Pencil and sheets of paper
Cautions	**Yes**. Negative feedback can open up personal issues. **PAL = L**
Variations	None
Process questions	**Yes**

Source: Adapted from Sue Forbes-Green, L.M.S.W.

EXERCISE I - 7 · DIMENSIONS OF TRUST

The purpose of this exercise is to facilitate healthy beliefs about trust and challenge cognitive distortions.

The facilitator engages participants in a group discussion about the word *"trust"* and what it means to them. Participants are asked to brainstorm actions and personal characteristics that build or promote trust. i.e., maintaining confidentiality, being dependable, caring manner, being understanding, etc. The list is put up on a board or flip chart. The group brainstorms specific things they can do at work to develop trust in others. The list is put up on a board or flip chart. The group then brainstorms those things that work against building trust, i.e., controlling others, lies, passive and aggressive behavior, etc. The list is put up on a board or flip chart. The group brainstorms specific things people do that work against developing trust in others. The list is put up on a board or flip chart.

PROCESS QUESTIONS:

Share a time when your trust was broken and what you felt and thought at that time.
Give an example of someone who broke your trust.
What makes it easy to trust others?
What makes it hard to trust others?

Purpose	Facilitate healthy beliefs and challenge cognitive distortions.
Level	**I**
Group size	**LG, SM**
Time ~ in minutes	30-60 minutes
Materials needed	Flip chart or dry erase board
Cautions	**Yes**. Can open up personal issues. **PAL = L**
Variations	None
Process questions	**Yes**

Source: Adapted from Sue Forbes-Green, L.M.S.W.

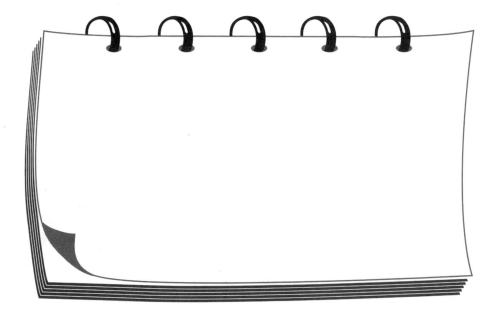

EXERCISE I - 8 · ON THE LEDGE

The purpose of this exercise is to facilitate trust building and self-exploration.

The facilitator divides participants into groups of four or five. Each group has a 16 foot piece of string to make a box about 3 x 5 feet. They are then told this represents a cliff's edge 300 feet above the ground, that they are all there for one night, and they will be rescued in the morning. They have to figure out how they will ALL sleep on the ledge without anyone falling off. If any group member's body extends over the line they are doomed. They have to arrange a position and hold it for three minutes.

PROCESS QUESTIONS:

What was your trust level? The Groups trust level?
What made you feel comfortable?
What made you feel uncomfortable?

Purpose	Facilitate trust building and self-exploration.
Level	**I**
Group size	**LG, SG**
Time ~ in minutes	5-10
Materials needed	Ball or string, large empty room or space
Cautions	**Yes**. Can open up personal issues. **PAL = M**
Variations	None
Process questions	**Yes**

Source: Sue Forbes-Green, L.M.S.W.

EXERCISE I - 9 · BODY CONSTRUCTION

The purpose of this exercise is to facilitate team work, group cohesion, and trust. For therapy groups the exercise can be used to develop a focus point to start a group session.

Participants are given simple instructions to use themselves to create a piece of playground equipment that will actually move when put all together. Participants are told they must demonstrate how the equipment works. Participants are given 5 minutes to discuss ideas and then are encouraged to begin to use themselves to form the piece of equipment. Once done the participants demonstrate how the piece of equipment works.

VARIATION:

Creativity is a must. Participants can create a variety of objects other than playground equipment

PROCESS QUESTIONS:

How does the equipment work?
If we were to remove one piece, what would happen?
What part is most important and where is it?
Identify this as the focal point and relate to the group process.

Purpose	Facilitate team work, group cohesion, and trust.
Level	**I**
Group size	**LG, SG**
Time ~ in minutes	10-15
Materials needed	Large open space
Cautions	None, **PAL = H**
Variations	**Yes**
Process questions	**Yes**

Source: Cindy Tyo, New Hope Treatment Centers

EXERCISE I - 10 · LEVELS OF DENIAL

The purpose of this exercise is to facilitate trust building, self-exploration, and self-disclosure.

There are things we tell strangers, things we share with colleagues, etc. but there are many things we would not tell anyone. We ask the patients with whom we work (and their families) to disclose very private and personal information. This exercise helps us explore how patients and families may feel.

The facilitator draws a small circle on a board or flip chart and writes the word "self" in the small circle. He/ she then draws a circle around that circle and writes the words "intimate friend/family member" inside that circle. The facilitator then draws three more circles/rings around the first two circles until the drawing looks like a bulls-eye.

In the third circle is written "friend," in the fourth is written "acquaintance," and in the outer circle is written "stranger."

The facilitator will pose several questions to the group, and one by one each group member answers the question by telling the group who they would share the answer with, a stranger, an acquaintance, a friend, an intimate, or keep it to him or her self (keep it a secret). For example if asked who would you tell what you had for breakfast this morning, most of us would probably be willing to tell anyone including a stranger, but if asked did your parent ever beat you with a strap, some of us might tell an intimate friend and others might not tell anybody (keep it a secret).

The facilitator asks the group the following question with the following statements:

Who would you tell...

Who you voted for?
That you have stolen something?
About the first time you ever had sex?
What your favorite color is?
That you have had an abortion? (for men, that you paid for your girlfriend to have an abortion)
How you are feeling today?
That you drank too much last night?
That you committed a felony?
That you are having sex with your boyfriend/girlfriend?

PROCESS QUESTIONS:

How did it feel to identify whom you would share certain thoughts with?
Was this exercise embarrassing for you? Why?

Purpose	Facilitate trust building, self-exploration, and self-disclosure
Level	**I**
Group size	**LG, SG**
Time ~ in minutes	15-30 minutes
Materials needed	Flip chart, black board, or dry erase board
Cautions	**Yes**. can open up personal issues and feelings. **PAL = L**
Variations	None
Process questions	**Yes**

EXERCISE I - 11 · PERSONAL SPACE

The purpose of this exercise is to help participants evaluate their boundaries and become aware of safe and unsafe boundaries.

Many patients have a poor sense of personal space and may not even be aware of or feel entitled to their own personal space. The facilitator divides the group into pairs. One participant slowly walks up to the other person in the pair who is standing still. The one standing still needs to tell the patient walking up to him/her when his/her personal space is being violated.

Different roles should be played with the "space invading" participant. For example, depending on one=s relationship with another person, an individual's personal space changes, i.e., a stranger is walking up to a person will result in the person maintaining a greater area of personal space and set limits if needed. The "space invading" person can play roles of a friend, acquaintance, family member, or stranger. The pairs then switch roles.

PROCESS QUESTIONS:

How did it feel to invade another's space?
How did it feel to have your space invaded?
Can you think of a time when someone invaded your personal space and it felt uncomfortable?

Purpose	To facilitate participants evaluation of their boundaries and become aware of safe and unsafe boundaries.
Level	**I**
Group size	**LG, SG, P**
Time ~ in minutes	5 -10 per pair
Materials needed	None
Cautions	None. **PAL = L**
Variations	None
Process questions	**Yes**

Source: Susan Robinson: Growing Beyond. NEARI Press

EXERCISE I - 12 · STINKING THINKING

The purpose of this exercise is to facilitate self-disclosure and reveal cognitive distortions that patients solidify in their minds.

Cognitive distortions (thinking errors) are the grease that keeps the cycle of any abusive behavior turning. Cognitive distortions are a critical part of illegal behaviors, aggressive situations, and self injurious situations such as shoplifting, vandalism, substance abuse, or eating disorders. Have participants divide into two or more groups. Each group has to come up with a list of as many cognitive distortions as possible. The cognitive distortions should apply to illegal behaviors, aggressive situations, and self injurious situations. When the group rejoins, the lists are shared. The group with the longest list wins.

VARIATION:

After the group lists are shared, they think of all the ways they can heal themselves in healthy ways and change their cognitive distortions, i.e., thought stopping, positive self-talk. Positive affirmations, etc. They make a group list of the beneficial things they can do and each group member receives a copy.

PROCESS QUESTIONS:

The group discusses all the different ways people attempt to feel better through quick and negative means, i.e., drugs, alcohol, promiscuous sex, etc. And the associated thinking errors.

Purpose	To facilitate self-disclosure and reveal cognitive distortions.
Level	**I**
Group size	**LG, SG**
Time ~ in minutes	20-30
Materials needed	Pencil and paper
Cautions	None. **PAL = L**
Variations	**Yes**
Process questions	**Yes**

Source: Susan Robinson: Growing Beyond. NEARI Press.

EXERCISE I - 13 · SHARING POSITIVE QUALITIES

The purpose of this exercise is to facilitate participants developing a better understanding of self, respect for self, appreciation for self, and build relationships among group members.

Many patients have low self-esteem, and a common treatment goal is to enhance it. In this exercise, each group member thinks of two positive qualities for each one of the other group members. Each group member gets a turn to hear all the positive qualities the group members say about him/her. One of the participants can be the note taker and make a separate list of the positive traits for each person, therefore, each participant can have his/her special list to think about and refer to when feeling bad.

Purpose	To facilitate participants developing a better understanding of self, respect for self, appreciation for self, and build relationships among group members.
Level	**I**
Group size	**LG, SG**
Time ~ in minutes	30 - 45
Materials needed	Paper and pencil
Cautions	None **PAL = L**
Variations	None
Process questions	Basic

Source: Susan Robinson: Growing Beyond. NEARI Press.

EXERCISE 1 - 14 · WHO WANTS TO BE A MILLIONAIRE

Based upon the popular television show "Who Wants to be a Millionaire", the purpose of this exercise is to improve the participants= knowledge base on core treatment issues.

This exercise is played like the television version except without real money awards. Each participant takes a turn being on the "hot seat" and answering questions that progress in difficulty. They can utilize group members for the three help options when they are stuck on a question: phone a friend (ask a group member), audience poll (poll the group), or 50-50 (take two of the incorrect answers away). The facilitator must have a series of questions in each subject category prepared before the exercise. Paper money can be used to enhance the game experience.

Subjects:

Human sexuality
Emotions
Empathy for others
Cognitive distortions
Friendships

VARIATION:

"Who Wants to be a Millionaire" II

Have the participants make up their own questions to challenge one another prior to doing the exercise.

Question Hat. The purpose of this exercise is to facilitate self-disclosure and comfort talking about difficult subjects.

Many patients are embarrassed to ask questions pertaining to sex or other difficult and personal issues because they fear their peers may laugh at them or think they are naïve. Participants anonymously write questions they have about sex or other topics. Each question is written on a small strip of paper which is then placed in a hat. The facilitator picks out questions, and answers and discusses the questions with the group to expand the participants' knowledge.

Topics:

Human sexuality
Friendships
Intimate relationships

PROCESS QUESTIONS:

What did you find easy to talk about?
What did you find hard to talk about?
Were you embarrassed doing this exercise? If so, why?

Purpose	To improve the participants' knowledge base on core treatment issues.
Level	**I**
Group size	**LG, SG**
Time ~ in minutes	10 per participant
Materials needed	Play money
Cautions	None **PAL = L**
Variations	**Yes**
Process questions	**Yes**

Source: Susan Robinson: Growing Beyond. NEARI Press.

EXERCISE I, M - 15 · FLASH CARDS

The purpose of this exercise to facilitate comfort in using words and to develop comfort with personal sharing. Depending on flash cards that are made and used, some participants can be triggered with flash card statements and/or responses by participants to the flash cards.

Participants sit in a circle. The facilitator uses a set of flash cards (see Appendix C), or make up beginning statements that are sentence completion. Each person in the group takes a turn completing the sentence. Examples for flash card statements:

My best friend…   Sometimes I think…
Sometimes I feel…   My mother…
No one….   Everyone…
I hate…   Christmas...
At night...   I'm afraid of...

See Appendix C for more flash card statements.

VARIATION:

Using props such as dolls or figurines, set up the room with a scene in the center before patients come in for group. Put together a still scene using dolls, figurines, etc. and then pick out one or two particular flash cards to set the scene. For example, put a female doll on the floor and a male doll on a chair next to her and set the flash card next to a chair leg that reads: "I remember feeling. . . The group comes in and is instructed to remain silent and study the still. The facilitator then asks the group to describe what they see.

PROCESS QUESTIONS:

Process group thoughts, feelings, and experience after going through the exercise.
What thoughts came to mind as you saw the flash cards?
What feelings did you experience after reading the flash cards?

Purpose	Facilitate self-disclosure
Level	**I, M**
Group size	**LG, SG, P, IC**
Time ~ in minutes	3-5 per person and flash card
Materials needed	Flash cards (Appendix B) or another suitable set.
Cautions	**Yes**. May trigger memories that are painful for some participants. **PAL = L**
Variations	**Yes**
Process questions	**Yes**

EXERCISE I, M - 16 · SCULPTURES

This exercise is similar to making "still" photographs using participants as props/characters in a photograph. The purpose of this exercise is to explore thoughts and feelings.

The facilitator has some options with this exercise. Participants can do several of the sample sculptures alone or in small groups. One participant can be appointed the "artist" for the sculpture or if in a group all can contribute to its design. Individual and small group work can be done simultaneously or one sculpture at a time in the center of the room. The facilitator selects one or more of the sample sculptures below and has each participant do an individual sculpture, selects several participants to make the sculpture, or can select one participant to make the sculpture who selects others to make it.

Sample sculptures:

There goes my ex girlfriend/boyfriend	You don't belong here
My family	This isn't safe
Get out	I'm not talking
I don't care	It wasn't me
Child abuse in the family	Death in the family

VARIATION:

Take one or more themes and have the participants do a before sculpture, i.e., what was happening before ("the setup"), a present sculpture ("dealing with the issue at the moment"), and an after sculpture ("what happens after/next").

PROCESS QUESTIONS:

As you made the sculpture what images came into mind?
What thoughts came up as you did the sculpture?
What feelings came up as you did the sculpture?
Has anything like this happened in your life?

Purpose	To facilitate exploration of thoughts and feelings, facilitate self-disclosure.
Level	**I, M**
Group size	**LG, SG**
Time ~ in minutes	5-10 per sculpture
Materials needed	Open space and some empty chairs
Cautions	**Yes**. Can open up thoughts and feelings, **PAL = M**
Variations	**Yes**
Process questions	**Yes**

EXERCISE I, M - 17 · COLOR BODY CHART

The purpose of this activity is to allow individuals an opportunity to express feelings non-verbally.

Participants are given a piece of paper with the outline of a body and a large selection of crayons. The participants are then instructed to select four colors to identify four different feelings. Once colors are selected they must draw a color key on the corner of the page identifying each feeling with a different color. Next, the participants are instructed to color the body using the chosen colors. The directive given is "color how you feel about yourself" (see variations below). Once the picture is completed, participants may be open to verbally discussing feelings by using the picture to describe.

VARIATIONS:

The directive's for coloring the picture can be of a large variety and may be used together in one session. Some of these may include:

"Color how you feel about (significant person)"
• your father
• your mother
• your brother
• your sister
• someone you have abused or hurt (use first name only)
• someone who has hurt or abused you (use first name only)

"Color how (significant person) feels about you."

PROCESS QUESTIONS:

Would you like to tell me about your drawing?
Can you tell me what you have done?

Purpose	Facilitate self-disclosure and express feelings.
Level	**I, M**
Group size	**LG, SG, P, IC**
Time ~ in minutes	5-10 for coloring
Materials needed	Paper, crayons, markers
Cautions	**Yes**. Can open up issues. **PAL = L**
Variations	**Yes**
Process questions	**Yes**

Source: Cindy Tyo, New Hope Treatment Centers

EXERCISE I, M - 18 · PILLOW TALK

The purpose of this exercise is to facilitate self-disclosure.

Children carry pillows for security. Teenagers select close friends to share secrets with. Adults share in bed at night. The facilitator instructs participants to come to group with a pillow or favorite stuffed animal (optional), or the facilitator brings in a pillow, which is passed around. The group sits in a circle. In a clockwise fashion beginning to the facilitator's left, each participant holds their pillow, stuffed animal or the pillow being passed around and takes a turn sharing something with the group about themselves.

PROCESS QUESTIONS:

When everyone is done, ask if anyone else has something more to share.
What was easy to share? Why?
What was hard to share? Why?
Is there more you would like to share?

Purpose	To facilitate self-disclosure.
Level	**I, M**
Group size	**LG, SG**
Time ~ in minutes	3-5 minutes per person
Materials needed	Pillows or stuffed animals (optional)
Cautions	**Yes**. Can open up personal issues. **PAL = L**
Variations	None
Process questions	**Yes**

Source: Adapted from Sue Forbess-Green, L.M.S.W.

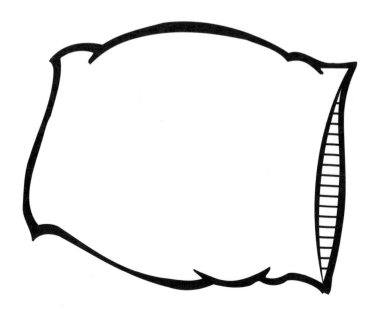

EXERCISE I, M - 19 · VICTIM'S EYES

The purpose of this exercise is to assist participants in using a written assignment to reach a feelings level, and to develop empathy and remorse.

The facilitator assigns participants to write a statement in the viewpoint of another person whom they hurt or abused. (The writing of this assignment evokes feeling, but by the time the individual presents the assignment to the group, the assignment is read without expression of feeling.) The written exercise is then done in a role-play.

The role-play requires a sheet, blanket, or any other partition to divide the group from one side of the room. Before the role-play starts another facilitator/staff member outside of the group (if possible) sits behind the partition (preferably without group members seeing who is sitting behind the partition). One of the written statements is given to the person behind the partition who in turn reads the assignment out loud. (The reader should be encouraged to read the paper with expression of feeling.)

PROCESS QUESTIONS:

How do participants feel as a group?
What do you feel about the person behind the partition?
What is different about this feeling and the one you were having at a time when you hurt or abused someone?

Purpose	Facilitate experiencing feelings, empathy and remorse.
Level	**I, M**
Group size	**LG, SG, P, IC**
Time ~ in minutes	20-30 written, 10-20 per role-play
Materials needed	Sheet or blanket, pencils and paper.
Cautions	**Yes**. Can open up personal issues, shame, and guilt. **PAL = M**
Variations	None
Process questions	**Yes**

Source: Cindy Tyo, New Hope Treatment Centers

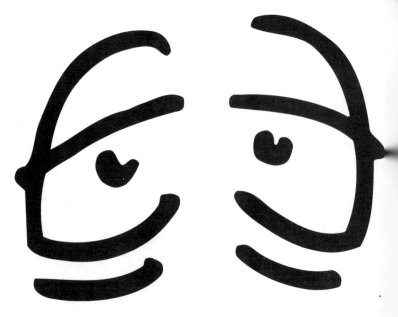

EXERCISE I, M - 20 · GUIDED IMAGERY THROUGH A CHILDHOOD HOME

The purpose of this exercise is to facilitate participants experiencing feelings related to an early childhood experience. These feelings may be both positive and difficult.

Facilitator instructs participants to find a safe place in the room. The facilitator instructs participants not to invade other's space and individuals can choose to close their eyes if they feel safe enough. Participants should get comfortable.

Participants are then guided by the facilitator to pay attention to his/her breathing in an effort to begin to relax. The instructor then continues to coach relaxation breathing for a short period of time, about 2-3 minutes. Once the participants appear to be relaxed, the instructor begins the guided imagery.

Journey: (Read slowly)

> Today we are going on a journey to a childhood home. Look down at your feet and you will see a circle of light hovering close to your ankles. When you are ready you can step onto the light and begin your journey home (pause). When you reach your home, carefully step off of the light, tell the light to wait for you and look around at your surroundings. What do you see? What do you hear? What do you feel? What do you smell? (pause) I want you to bend down and touch the ground. Is it cold or warm? Is it soft or hard? Now, slowly stand up and when you are ready I want you to go to the door. Make note of the handle. Is it cold or warm? Is it locked or unlocked? Do you have a key? With or without a key the door opens and you can now enter the house.

> Once inside, stop at the door and look all around you. What do you hear? What do you smell? What do you see? What do you feel? Now I want you to begin to journey through your home. Remember the light is waiting outside for you and you can return at any time. I want you to walk through every room. See what you can see, hear what you can hear, smell what you can smell, and feel what you can feel (longer pause). When you are ready, go back outside, take one last look (pause), step onto the light, and return back to the here and now. When you are ready, slowly open your eyes and return to the group.

> Once all participants are ready, the group facilitator instructs participants to draw the floor plan of the house they just journeyed through. Participants are encouraged to include all sensory observations. What did you see, hear, smell, feel, or even taste?

PROCESS QUESTIONS:

How would you describe this experience?
If you could have brought something back with you, what would you have brought? How are you feeling now?
Did you want to leave or stay? Why?

VARIATION:

Journey to a childhood playground. In this imagery the participants might be guided to imagine the playground empty except for one small child. As they look closer they realize the child is him/her self at a much younger age. One could guide the participants to speak to the child for a short while.

PROCESS QUESTIONS:

What did you see?
How were you feeling?
How was the child feeling?
What did you say to the child?
What was the child's response?
How did you leave the child?

Purpose	Facilitate participants experiencing feelings related to an early childhood experience.
Level	**I, M**
Group size	**LG, SG**
Time ~ in minutes	10-20 minutes
Materials needed	Open space for participants to relax in
Cautions	**Yes**. Can open up personal issues. **PAL = L**
Variations	**Yes**
Process questions	**Yes**

Source: Cindy Tyo, New Hope Treatment Centers

CHAPTER FIVE ~ INTERMEDIATE LEVEL EXERCISES

EXERCISE M - 1 · MY PAPER DOLL

The purpose of this exercise is to facilitate self-exploration.

Each participant is given a large sheet (6-7 foot long) of rolled newspaper print paper (or tape two sheets from a flip chart together end to end). A variety of pens, pencils, markers, crayons, etc. are provided to the group. Each participant lays down on the paper and another participant makes an outline of the participant's body on the paper (use pencil to avoid damage to clothing). When everyone has an outline of their body each participant then begins to mark their outline with personal strengths and weaknesses. Participants can color, add particular organs (i.e., heart, facial features, etc.) to their body outline.

VARIATIONS:

Participants can identify particular problems they are experiencing and note where the problem manifests itself physically in their body, i.e., worry can be in the stomach, stress in the head or shoulders, etc.

Participants can work in pairs and help each other explore and identify strengths and weaknesses, where problems manifest themselves physically.

Use the Chakra Chart (Appendix D) to compare one's problems to the corresponding part of the body on the chakra chart and identify corresponding physical ailments.

Draw a line down the center of the body drawing. Make the left side the "Old Me" and the right side the "New Me." Use the left side (old me to list personal problems, deficits and weaknesses and the right side to label strengths, goals, and personal changes made or to make. Source: (Jim Haaven, Personal Communication).

PROCESS QUESTIONS:

How easy was it to identify your strengths and why?
How easy was it to identify your weaknesses and why?
Can you relate problems you experience to physical ailments your experience?

Purpose	Facilitate self exploration
Level	**M**
Group size	**LG, SG, P, IC**
Time ~ in minutes	15-20 minutes
Materials needed	Large roll of sheets of paper, pencils, pens, markers, crayons
Cautions	**Yes**. Can open up personal issues. **PAL = L**
Variations	**Yes**
Process questions	**Yes**

EXERCISE M - 2 · SIGNIFICANT EVENTS

The purpose of this exercise is to facilitate self-disclosure and personal insight.

This is a mime exercise. Participants are placed in groups of 6-12, standing in a circle. Taking no more than 20-30 seconds, each participant gets into center of circle and demonstrates (mimes) a significant event from their life, without talking (this is similar to charades). The group tries to guess what the event was.

VARIATION:

Ask the person to describe the circumstances around the event without saying what the event was.

If you have a variety of masks that portray different feelings, the participant puts on a mask and then mimes an event and the group has to guess what happened (the problem) and what the person is feeling.

PROCESS QUESTIONS:

What is it like to communicate without using words?
What was hard about this exercise?
What did you learn about yourself?
What did you learn about others?

Purpose	Facilitate self-disclosure and personal insight.
Level	**M**
Group size	**LG, SG**
Time ~ in minutes	1-2 minutes per participant
Materials needed	None
Cautions	**Yes**. May open up personal issues and problems. **PAL = L/M**
Variations	**Yes**
Process questions	**Yes**

EXERCISE M - 3 · ARGUMENTS

The purpose of this exercise is to facilitate self-expression and work on anger control.

Group participants sit in a circle. The trainer initiates a group discussion about the various ways in which people tend to argue with each other. How does arguing tie into anger and personal ways of expressing anger? How do we deal with disagreements and arguments with other staff/patients? Two participants at a time are selected and stand in the center of the circle. They are instructed to have an argument. They select a topic or the trainer/group facilitator gives them an argument topic. They are instructed to argue with one of the following stipulations.

• argue with no restrictions
• argue but they cannot use swear words
• argue with their hands in pockets

VARIATIONS:

Where do you draw the line? Many of us have a point beyond which we may tell the truth and deny a particular action or behavior. Explore with the group who would deny to a parent or spouse that they 1) got a parking ticket, 2) got a speeding ticket for $200, 3) had a car accident and in fact it was your fault, and 4) had an affair or got a woman pregnant.

Two participants stand in the center of the circle and have an argument, one person is instructed to use one of the following types of denial. A subject for the argument is given by the facilitator/trainer.

• complete outright denial
• denial of denial: denial that you are denying the problem
• denial of responsibility for your behavior
• denial of intention to do a particular act or behavior
• denial of the frequency you have engaged in a particular behavior
• denial of harm to the person you acted out against
• denial of violence or aggression
• denial of facts about what you have done
• denial of planning your behavior

PROCESS QUESTIONS:

What was hard about this exercise?
What did you learn about yourself?
What did you learn about others?

Purpose	Facilitate inter-personal skills, anger expression, self-disclosure, trust.
Level	**M**
Group size	**LG, SG, P, IC**
Time ~ in minutes	10 minutes per pair
Materials needed	None
Cautions	**Yes**. May open up personal issues and emotions. **PAL = M**
Variations	**Yes**
Process questions	**Yes**

EXERCISE M - 4 · ROLE THROW-AWAY

The purpose of this exercise is to facilitate self-disclosure and personal insight.

Participants sit in a circle. Each has paper and pencil. The paper is folded in half and then half again so it has four quarters. Participants are to write FOUR roles they assume in their lives that are important; i.e., patient, child, student, friend, athlete, etc.

Each person takes a turn briefly discussing his/her roles with the group. After a group discussion each participant tears off one role and throws it in the box in the center of circle.

Each participant takes a turn to discuss how it would feel if he/she could really throw away one role in his/her life.

VARIATION:

Repeat the exercise with all four roles.

PROCESS QUESTIONS:

What would be the impact of throwing away a life role?
What would be difficult about throwing away a life role?
What would be different to not have the associated responsibilities and demands of that role?

Purpose	Facilitate self-disclosure and personal insight.
Level	**M**
Group size	**LG, SG, P, IC**
Time ~ in minutes	8 -10 minutes per person
Materials needed	Paper, pen or pencil, small box (i.e., shoe box)
Cautions	**Yes**. can open up personal issues, problems, emotions. **PAL = L**
Variations	**Yes**
Process questions	**Yes**

EXERCISE M - 5 · HOT POTATO

The purpose of this exercise is to facilitate self-disclosure, personal sharing, and self-expression.

Participants sit in a circle. They are given a foam ball or soft light object like a wiffle ball to throw back and forth to each other. The facilitator puts on a music tape or CD. When the music is playing participants throw the foam ball to avoid having it (like a hot potato). When the music stops, participants stop throwing the ball and the person in possession of the ball has to answer a question.

Sample questions:

How do you feel today?
What makes you feel scared?
What bothers you most?
What angers you most?
What was the most embarrassing situation you experienced?
What is the biggest lie you ever told?
What is the worst thing that has ever happened to you?

VARIATION:

With a collection of masks, the person with the ball has to pick a mask out of the pile and describe the feeling on the mask and then relate it to his/her life in some way. Continue until all masks have been used.

PROCESS QUESTIONS:

What was most difficult about this exercise?
What was the hardest feeling or thought for you to share with others? Why?

Purpose	Facilitate self-disclosure, personal sharing, and self-expression.
Level	**M**
Group size	**LG, SM, P, IC**
Time ~ in minutes	5 per person
Materials needed	Foam ball or wiffle ball, tape or CD player, music
Cautions	**Yes**. May open up personal issues, problems, and emotions. **PAL = L**
Variations	**Yes**
Process questions	**Yes**

Source: L. Lowestein

EXERCISE M - 6 · PERSONAL DILEMMAS

The purpose of this exercise is to facilitate exploration of personal, morals, values and beliefs.

The facilitator makes up a set of personal dilemma questions or uses dilemmas from the list below. Participants sit in a circle and one by one the facilitator reads each dilemma out loud to the group. The facilitator asks for volunteers to respond to each dilemma by answering whether each dilemma poses a violation of another's trust, a personal value and/or belief, moral, etc. and why.

It is important that the facilitator does not give any more information or read anything into the personal dilemmas. Many are vague and designed to be confusing.

VARIATION:

Each participant writes down on a slip of paper their name and their answer to each dilemma and notes the dilemma with their answer, i.e., dilemma 3-no, dilemma 7-yes. Participants turn in their answers to the facilitator. The facilitator randomly selects slips of paper and the participant has to discuss his/her answer and why he/she answered that way.

Each participant has to share their answer for each dilemma with the group.

Sample personal dilemmas:

1. A long-time and very close friend brings you a gift. The friend tells you that he/she stole it.

2. A friend asks you if he/she can make a copy of a paper you turned in for a class last year so he/she can turn it in for a class assignment tomorrow.

3. You see another student from your school take something from another person's locker.

4. You see your friend take a piece of paper (or stack of papers) from the teacher's desk at school and replace it with another piece of paper (or stack of papers).

5. A friend asks you to smoke some marijuana.

6. A girl's dress is unbuttoned/boy's pants are unzipped and you can see her brassier/his underwear. You stare at her/him and don't say a word.

7. The person you are dating is pressuring you to have sex and you don't want to. He/she is not of legal age.

PROCESS QUESTIONS:

The facilitator processes the exercise with the participants and asks the following questions regarding the above dilemmas.

Which of the dilemmas above, might be harmful to you/the other person?
Which of the dilemmas above involve personal morals, values, and beliefs?
To which dilemmas would you answer "it depends" or " I need more information."
Would your response depend on who else knew or didn't know?

Purpose	Facilitate exploration of personal morals, values, and beliefs.
Level	**M**
Group size	**LG, SG, P, IC**
Time ~ in minutes	5-10 minutes per person
Materials needed	Paper, pencils or pens.
Cautions	**Yes**. May open up personal issues and emotional responses. **PAL = L**
Variations	**Yes**
Process questions	**Yes**

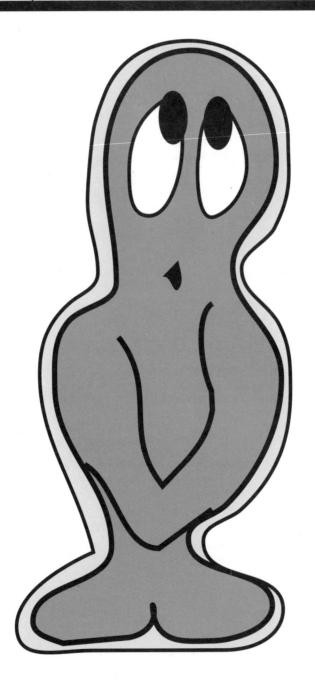

EXERCISE M - 7 · THE COCKTAIL PARTY

The purpose of this exercise is to facilitate self-disclosure and explore values and belief systems.

Patients are divided into small groups or 4-6 people. Each group is instructed to pretend that they have become one of their parents. They are at a cocktail party talking with others. The topic of the conversation is their children. So now, each participant is at a party in the role of their parent talking about him/her self (their son/daughter).

VARIATION:

Using the exercise above, patients pretend they are their school teacher, or therapist (remind patients that in a real life scenario, it is unethical for teachers or therapists to discuss students or patients with others without permission).

PROCESS QUESTIONS:

What was it like to pretend to be your parent and go inside your parent's head?
How honest were you?
Why did you choose to talk about yourself in the way you did?
What issue(s) did you avoid talking about in relationship to yourself?

Purpose	To facilitate self-disclosure and explore values and belief systems.
Level	**M**
Group size	**LG, SG**
Time ~ in minutes	10 -15 per exercise
Materials needed	None
Cautions	**Yes**. May open up personal issues and emotional responses. **PAL = L**
Variations	**Yes**
Process questions	**Yes**

Source: Adapted from John Bergman; Geese Theatre Company

EXERCISE M - 8 · EVALUATION

The purpose of this exercise is to facilitate understanding and awareness about how participants present themselves to others (their outer self).

The facilitator instructs participants to rate each of the other group members on a 1-5 scale on personal responsibility. 1 = they have no personal responsibility, 2 = almost no personal responsibility, 3 = some personal responsibility, 4 = average personal responsibility, and 5 = is very personally responsible. They then discuss ways to improve being responsible. The group is instructed and agrees to provide one another with constructive and appropriate feedback only. No negative criticism is allowed. <u>Note</u>: This exercise should not be done unless the group is **safe**, honest, sensitive to one another's needs, and cohesive. When this is the case, it is a mutually supportive and encouraging exercise.

VARIATIONS:

Using the exercise above, have participants rate each other on the following characteristics:

Honesty
Trustworthiness
Empathy
Care for others
Respect for others
Self-worthiness

Participants are given a pad and paper to write their evaluations of others and ratings are shared after the discussion on the personal characteristic.

PROCESS QUESTIONS:

What was it like to hear others feedback?
Did you agree with the feedback?
If you do not agree what do you not agree with?

Purpose	To facilitate understanding and awareness about how participants present themselves to others.
Level	**M**
Group size	**LG, SG**
Time ~ in minutes	30-45 minutes
Materials needed	Pencil and paper
Cautions	**Yes**. May open up personal issues and emotional responses. **PAL = L**
Variations	**Yes**
Process questions	**Yes**

EXERCISE M - 9 · HEALTHY VS. UNHEALTHY RELATIONSHIPS

The purpose of this exercise is to facilitate self-exploration, self-disclosure, and trust in others.

Many patients have dysfunctional relationships and a limited understanding about healthy ones. The facilitator divides participants into two groups, and has them consider and discuss the qualities of each. Participants write lists of the differences. When the group rejoins, the participants talk about the unhealthy and healthy relationships they have seen in their lives, and been involved in.

VARIATION I:

The Key to Friendships

Many patients have attachment difficulties, limited friendships, and poor social skills. The purpose of this exercise is to help them better understand what friendships entail. The participants discuss the following:

What does it mean to be a friend, what are the attributes friends possess?
What are the signs of healthy and unhealthy friendships, and how do you show someone that you care?

After the discussion the participants make lists based on the ideas above and each group member is provided a copy that they can consult for guidance.

VARIATION II:

Healthy vs. Unhealthy Boundaries

Many patients have extremely poor boundaries due to their own trauma, abuse issues, and life experiences. Helping them understand boundaries is imperative. This exercise is conducted the same manner as the one above: the group is divided into two and the patients explore, discuss, and write out the qualities of healthy and unhealthy boundaries. When the group rejoins, the girls talk about the unhealthy and healthy boundaries they have seen in their lives, and which boundaries they currently possess.

VARIATION III:

Healthy vs. Unhealthy Sexuality

The purpose of this exercise is to enhance the group=s awareness and understanding of healthy and unhealthy sexuality. As with previous exercises, the group is divided into two and the participants explore, discuss, and write out the qualities of healthy and unhealthy sexuality. When the group rejoins, the participants talk about their own sexuality and what specifically has been, or currently is, healthy or unhealthy about it. They can also discuss what they learned from their home environments about sexuality and if they received healthy or unhealthy sexual role modeling.

PROCESS QUESTIONS:

The group discusses the three different boundary styles: non-existent, walled, or healthy.

Which boundary do you most often adopt for yourself?
Discuss the pros and cons of choosing that style. Option: Group members provide feedback to one another on how each group member presents him/her self to see if their self-assessments match each group members' assessment.

Purpose	To facilitate self-exploration, self-disclosure, and trust in others.
Level	**M**
Group size	**LG, SG**
Time ~ in minutes	20 - 30
Materials needed	Pencil and paper
Cautions	**Yes**. Can open up personal issues. **PAL = L**
Variations	**Yes**
Process questions	**Yes**

Source: Susan Robinson: Growing Beyond. NEARI Press.

EXERCISE M, A - 10 · LIFE COLLAGE

The purpose of this exercise is to facilitate self-expression, and personal self-disclosure.

Facilitator brings to the group of participants a variety of materials to make a collage. Each person is given a 18"X24" or 24"X36" piece of poster board upon which to build their collage. The facilitator suggests to participants that they can use whatever materials they want. The facilitator gives the group of participants a theme for the collage project.

Examples of collage themes:

My Life
My Career
My Family
My Past
My Future
My Secrets
My Treatment Issues

VARIATION:

Participants can select his/her own theme for his/her collage.
The group of participants does one large group collage together.

PROCESS QUESTIONS:

What personal issues came up for you as you did your collage?
Why did you choose the theme of your collage?
What was fun about this project?
What was most difficult about this project?
What did you learn about yourself?
What did you learn about others?

Purpose	Facilitate self-expression, and personal self-disclosure.
Level	**M, A**
Group size	**LG, SG, P, IC**
Time ~ in minutes	60
Materials needed	Poster board, crayons, pens, pencils, scissors, magazines, newspapers, glue, tape, and decorations (glitter, ribbons, etc.)
Cautions	**Yes**. May open up personal issues and problems and emotions. **PAL = L**
Variations	**Yes**
Process questions	**Yes**

EXERCISE M, A - 11 · INTRODUCE YOUR PARTNER

The purpose of this exercise is to facilitate personal disclosure, trust, building relationships.

Participants pair off with someone they don't know or know well. Each pair has to find out three pieces of information about the person he/she has paired off with, the person's name and his/her age or weight, and two additional facts about the person (See topics list below.) Each participant takes a turn reporting to the group what they learned about the person he/she paired off with.

Topics to explore in paired discussions:

A family rule you have broken
A law you have broken
A secret you did not keep
A personal secret
Something few people know about you
My biggest fear
The person I love more than anyone

VARIATION:

Do the same exercise in groups of three
Participants have the choice to share what they feel safe sharing with the entire group

PROCESS QUESTIONS:

What was fun about this exercise?
What was hard about this exercise?
What was most difficult to share? Why?
What did you learn about yourself?
What did you learn about the other person?

Purpose	Facilitate personal disclosure, trust, building relationships.
Level	**M, A**
Group size	**LG, SG**
Time ~ in minutes	5-10 minutes per pair
Materials needed	None
Cautions	**Yes**. May open up emotions, personal issues and personal problems. **PAL = L**
Variations	**Yes**
Process questions	**Yes**

EXERCISE M, A - 12 · PERSONAL STORY

The purpose of this exercise is to facilitate personal disclosure, trust, and building relationships.

Participants pair off and share a personal story with each other that they have not told anyone or many other people. The facilitator oversees the exercise but there is no group sharing about the story and process questions are optional.

VARIATION:

Participants take turns sharing their partner's story with the rest of the group.
Exercise is repeated with groups of three.

PROCESS QUESTIONS:

Why did you select your personal story?
What was hard about sharing it?
What feelings came up as you told your story?
Was the story 100% complete?

Purpose	Facilitate personal disclosure, trust, building relationships.
Level	**M, A**
Group size	**LG, SG**
Time ~ in minutes	10-20 minutes
Materials needed	None
Cautions	**Yes**. May open up emotions, issues or personal problems. **PAL = L**
Variations	**Yes**
Process questions	**Yes**

CHAPTER SIX - ADVANCED EXERCISES

EXERCISE A - 1 · PERSONAS

The purpose of this exercise is to facilitate self-disclosure, trust, and personal sharing.

In order to do this exercise the facilitator will need to have a variety of masks, preferably professionally made masks, that represent a variety of feelings and emotions, i.e., silly, sad, happy, anger, anxiety, depression, confused, rage, concerned, content, etc. (For resources see Appendix E).

The facilitator explains to participants that most of us have at least three personas; our public/current persona (the person we are in public around others), our private or secret persona (the part of us few if any people know about), and our future persona (the person we see ourselves being in the future). Each persona has many feelings or emotions attached to it.

Masks are placed in the middle of the floor and participants are instructed to pick one mask that best represents their private/secret persona/self. After each person selects a mask, the facilitator encourages volunteers to share why they chose that mask and the feeling(s) it represents.

VARIATION:

All participants are required to share in group.
Repeat the exercise with public persona and/or future persona.
Contrast one's private vs. public persona.

PROCESS QUESTIONS:

Why did you choose the particular mask?
What feeling is most closely associated with the mask you chose?

Purpose	Facilitate self-disclosure, trust, and personal sharing.
Level	**A**
Group size	**LG, SG, P**
Time ~ in minutes	5-10 per person
Materials needed	Masks
Cautions	**Yes**. May open up emotions, personal issues, and problems. **PAL = L**
Variations	**Yes**
Process questions	**Yes**

EXERCISE A - 2 · WHAT AM I SUPPOSED TO DO?

The purpose of this exercise is to facilitate self-exploration, skills development, self-exploration, self-confidence, and self-disclosure.

Based on the popular TV show 2002 with Drew Carey, "What's My Line Anyway", the facilitator comes up with various vignettes, situations, role-plays, etc. and participants have to use impromptu role-plays and/or mime. Humor is welcome.

The facilitator encourages impromptu role-play and the use of props (optional) such as masks, hats, dolls, toys, gadgets, etc. The facilitator picks two or more participants to role-play a vignette. Sample vignettes are listed below.

Sample vignettes:

1. You are at the beach and go into the ocean. As you swim the strong current pulls off the bottom of your bikini/swim trunks. Your towel is about 30 feet from the water but there are several other people around both in the water and on the beach. Get your towel without anyone seeing you naked.

2. You are about to ask someone you really like at school to the prom. You are having a conversation with that person when another student comes up and asks him/her if they have a date for the prom yet? Ask him/her before the other person does.

3. You are walking your dog when you bump into this person you really like. You are about ready to ask him/her if he/she is free to go to a movie on Friday night. You look down to discover your dog has lifted his leg and is peeing all over that person's shoes. Make the date for Friday night.

4. Your on a date and in the theater watching a romantic movie. You lean over to give your date a kiss. Just as you lean over you pass gas. It doesn't make any noise but it really smells. Convince your date that it wasn't you so you can get the kiss you want.

5. You're at school with your best friend. A groups of kids comes up and teases/picks on him because they saw his name on the sex offender registry. This is the first time you hear about/know about your friend and that he has committed a sex offense. Stand up for your friend.

PROCESS QUESTIONS:

What was easy for you to do?
What was difficult for you to do?
What did you learn about yourself?
What did you learn about others?

Purpose	Facilitate self-exploration, skills development, self exploration, self-confidence, and self-disclosure.
Level	**A**
Group size	**LG, SG**
Time ~ in minutes	3-5 minutes per exercise
Materials needed	Large open space, props for vignettes (optional).
Cautions	**Yes**. May open up personal issues, problems, and emotions. **PAL = M/H**
Variations	None
Process questions	**Yes**

EXERCISE A - 3 · SEXUAL MISCONDUCT

The purpose of this exercise is to facilitate self-exploration of personal boundaries, values, morals, and beliefs regarding sexual behavior.

One of the growing concerns with young people is their involvement in sexually inappropriate behavior, sexual harassment, and/or sexual misconduct. Personal boundaries must be considered when looking at sexual behavior, and one's family, culture, and community values can influence one's sexual attitudes and beliefs. Our sexual values, morals, attitudes and beliefs help guide and govern our sexual behavior.

The facilitator leads the participants through the following exercise:

Certain scenarios can lead to inappropriate sexual behavior or sexual harassment/misconduct between two persons. The facilitator makes a list of sexual scenarios or uses the sample list below. Which of the scenarios is problematic sexual behavior and why? On a piece of paper, write the numbers 1-10 in a column. As each scenario is read, write "yes" beside the number if the example given is inappropriate sexual behavior, sexual misconduct or sexual abuse. Write "no" if it is normal, consenting, and/or appropriate behavior. If the answer is "yes" indicate whether the behavior is inappropriate, sexual harassment, or sexual abuse.

Sample scenarios:

1. Holding hands with your girlfriend/boyfriend at school.
2. Showing a playboy picture of a nude woman to a 13-year-old.
3. Telling jokes about large-breasted women in front of other girls and boys.
4. Commenting about the "bulge" in some guy's pants.
5. Giving frequent hugs to girls /boys you don't know that well.
6. Wearing promiscuous clothing to school/work.
7. Sexual talk in front of a younger sibling 12 years old or younger.
8. Telling personal sexual experiences in front of girls/boys at school.
9. Walking up to a girl/boy and putting your hand on her breasts/crotch.
10. Staring at someone in their bathing suit and commenting on her nice boobs/his nice bulge.

PROCESS QUESTIONS:

What is difficult about determining which of the scenarios is appropriate, inappropriate, harassment or abusive?
What harm can be caused to the people involved?
To which would you answer "it depends" or " I need more information"?
Does it make a difference if the person in the scenario is male or female?
Does it make a difference if the person is a lot younger or a lot older than you?
Does it make a difference if the person is considered to be attractive vs. unattractive?

Purpose	Facilitate self-exploration of personal boundaries, values, morals, and beliefs regarding sexual behavior.
Level	**A**
Group size	**LG, SG, P, IC**
Time ~ in minutes	60
Materials needed	Pencil, pen, paper, black board, dry erase board or flip chart.
Cautions	**Yes**. can open up personal issues and problems. **PAL = L**
Variations	None
Process questions	**Yes**

EXERCISE A - 4 · PAIRED SCULPTURES

The purpose of this exercise is to assist participants in becoming comfortable with movement and touch.

Participants are paired off. Each pair is labeled person "A" and person "B." The facilitator demonstrates sculpting a person from the group as if he/she is a chunk of clay. This can be done with as much detail as participants feel comfortable doing with each other, using fingers, facial expressions, etc. Sculpting is done in complete silence. Person A goes first and sculpts person B.

VARIATIONS:

Participants take turns sculpting each other (swap A & B in sculpting role).

Participants in the group can guess what the sculpture is when each pair is done, i.e., teacher, athlete, etc. What does each sculpture have in common? What do they like about the sculpture? etc.

Ask each pair after a sculpting is complete, "What's the Story?"

Have two people or more sculpt a scene or story using as many participants from the group as necessary. Ask the group what's the story?

Arguments The facilitator asks the group for examples of arguments. Who is involved? Where does it take place? Over what? Then the facilitator selects two volunteers and the group positions them (sculpts them) into a sculpture of an argument without saying or discussing what the argument is. The group can tell them where to stand or can physically move them. The facilitator then asks the participants to guess, "What is the story?"

PROCESS QUESTIONS:

What comes to mind as you sculpt another person?
What comes to mind as another person sculpts you?
What memories did you have as you watched sculptures being done? What thoughts/feelings did you experience?

Purpose	Facilitates self-disclosure. Opens up issues to be worked on in treatment.
Level	**A**
Group size	**LG, SG, P**
Time ~ in minutes	5-10 per sculpting activity
Materials needed	None
Cautions	**Yes**. Exercise should be debriefed as it can open up personal issues to be worked on in treatment. **PAL = M**
Variations	**Yes**
Process questions	**Yes**

Source: John Bergman, Geese Theatre Company

EXERCISE A - 5 · ROLE-PLAY

The purpose of this exercise is to help patients develop appropriate assertiveness, manage anger, and work with healthy thinking.

The facilitator develops a list of real life scenarios or can draw from the list of sample scenarios below. The facilitator plays the role of the other person in the selected scenario and the participant plays him/her self. The scenario for the role-play should be one that creates a conflict and is a difficult (uncomfortable) situation for the participant to address. The facilitator in his/her role will be resistant, difficult, and even rude (but not impossible). The participant practices doing the role-play several times until he/she can work out the problem with the authority figure.

Role-play scenarios:

Ask Dad to borrow the car (i.e., to take friends to a movie, to go out on a date, etc.).
Late for a therapy session.
Late from meeting with probation officer.
Did not turn in homework project on time.
Need to borrow money from a parent.
Meeting with principle for skipping school.

Advanced role-play scenarios:

Confronting an abuser.
Confronting an abusive parent.
Confronting a friend who lied, cheated, was unfaithful, or stole.
Being confronted by someone you hurt or abused.

VARIATION:

Make the role-play impossible, that is the participant does not get what he/she wants (i.e., the car) or is not excused (i.e., being late) and/or has to deal with a consequence.

After role-play have participants swap roles.

PROCESS QUESTIONS:

Debrief role-play with patient and group members who observed. Feedback from group members is optional.

Purpose	Cognitive restructuring, emotional development.
Level	**A**
Group size	**LG, SG, P, IC**
Time ~ in minutes	5-10
Materials needed	None
Cautions	**Yes**. May trigger anger and other psychological problems. **PAL = M**
Variations	**Yes**
Process questions	**Yes**

EXERCISE A - 6 · EMPATHY FOR SELF AND OTHERS

Many patients come into treatment with a history of abuse; physical, psychological, sexual, and emotional. These patients have difficulty trusting others. The purpose of the exercises below is to facilitate self-disclosure, enhance self-confidence, and work on developing healthy emotions, self-empathy and empathy for others.

Overcoming Victimhood

Many victims of sexual abuse adopt a victim stance for themselves. They view the world with a tainted lens that results in a negative worldview and a belief that people are out to hurt them. The purpose of this exercise is to change the lens to one that is more efficacious, one that alters a victim stance to a survivor/thriver stance. Helping group members understand how to overcome obstacles is important and the girls can share with one another how they have done this in their own lives. They can also be encouraging to those group members who adopt more of a victim stance by identifying and discussing strengths that are developed as a result of trauma.

The Secret Garden

Abuse victims often internalize destructive messages about their own abuse, i.e., they must have deserved it. Because of the level of shame accompanied by these messages, patients often keep these harmful thoughts secret. In this exercise, the group discusses all the unhealthy secrets abuse victims can adopt as a result of abuse. They then examine and dispel these secrets, and rewrite them to counter the negative internalized beliefs, i.e., "I didn't stop the abuse so I must have like it" is changed to "I didn't fight because if I fought back, I thought he might hurt me or my family."

Positive Self-Talk

Because many of these patients have spent much of their time engaging in negative self-talk, it is important for them to learn how to counter these negative messages and rewrite a healthier script. In this exercise, the patients brainstorm and write an extensive list of all the negative messages they give themselves. This is a group list and each group member shares his/her particular negative messages to add to the list. The more ridiculous these messages are the better so they can realize how silly some of them are. The group members then help one another combat these negative messages. This is a good exercise to normalize these negative messages and understand how our culture may influence patients' thinking; for example, "I must be gay," "I'm too fat" or "I'm not sexy enough" are messages often derived from cultural scripts. It can also be an empowering exercise for the patients because they realize the unhealthy beliefs they have adopted, and start challenging those beliefs instead of blindly accepting them.

Crumpled Paper
Source: Adapted from Victory Peterson, LMSW, PPO III, 6th Judicial District Department of Correctional Services Cedar Rapids, IA."

Using colored paper ask the group members to think of the person they love most in the world, select a sheet of paper and write their name at the top of the paper. Then, below the name, they list all the things they love about that person. They should fill up the sheet -- all the things that make the person dear to them. Then, when they have all laid their pencils down, instruct them to crumple the piece of paper up into as tight a ball as possible. They may look surprised and a little bit offended by this, but encourage them to really wad it up tightly. After they have done so, ask them to spread the paper out again and work out all the wrinkles. They will work at this for a minute or so and it's kind of interesting to watch their faces. Tell them this is what victimization does to the individual they offended against. No matter how hard they try, the paper can never again be flat and unlined. The paper still exists, the person still exists and all the qualities there are still part of the person but something has been added that can never be taken away. Have the patients keep their pieces of paper in their notebooks. Every several months have them take the piece of paper out and talk about the piece of paper again

Impact of Abuse

Although many of these patients may have experienced abuse in their histories, it is also true they may have difficulty articulating the impact of such abuse. Understanding abuse impact helps build empathy; if they begin to comprehend the impact of abuse in general, they can start applying this knowledge to their own history of abuse and to their victim(s). In this exercise, the group is divided into two teams. Each team creates a list of all the *thoughts* sexual abuse victim's experience. The group with the longest list wins. The differences and commonalities among the lists are reviewed as well. The patients also write separate lists for the *feelings* and *behaviors* that victim's experience. This will help group members better differentiate between thoughts, feelings, and behaviors.

Voices of Victims

Source: Pat Van Buren, North Carolina

Each group usually starts with a sampling of victim materials including art, poems, books, videos, etc. Keep an empty chair in the room in honor of all the victims.

The following poem was sent to an incest father by his 13 yr. old victim
before he started treatment. She told him in the letter that each time she
visited him in prison she felt so dirty she had to go home and take a bath.

WHICH?
I watched them tearing a building down,
A gang of men in a busy town.
With a "Yo-heave-ho" and a lusty yell,
They swung a beam and a side wall fell.
I asked the foreman,
"Are these men as skilled as the men you'd hire
if you had to build?
He gave a laugh and said,
"No indeed! Just common labor is all I need.
I can easily wreck in a day or two what builders have taken years to do."
I thought to myself as I went my way,
"Which of these games have I tried to play?"
Am I a builder who works with care,
Measuring life by the rule and square
Am I shaping my deeds to a well laid plan
Patiently doing the best I can?"
or
"Am I a wrecker who walks the town,
Content with the labor of tearing down?"

PROCESS QUESTIONS:

Name the positives and negatives of trusting others, and the importance of taking risks.
What does trust mean to each group member?
How do you learn to trust others?
How do you know when someone can be trusted?
Have each participant assess whether or not she is trustworthy. What can she/he do to become more trustworthy?

Each participant discusses her/his own willingness to trust or her/his current level of distrust.

Purpose	Facilitate self-disclosure, enhance self-confidence, and work on developing healthy emotions, self-empathy and empathy for others.
Level	**A**
Group size	**LG, SG, P, IC**
Time ~ in minutes	30 or more
Materials needed	Pencils, pens, paper, colored paper, assorted readings.
Cautions	**Yes**. May open up issues and emotional responses. **PAL = L**
Variations	**Yes**
Process questions	**Yes**

Source: Susan Robinson: Growing Beyond. NEARI Press (Except where otherwise noted).

REFERENCES

Bartleson, M. (2001). James Island County Recreation. Personal Communication.

Bays, L. and Freeman-Longo, R.E. (2000) Enhancing empathy. Holyoke, MA: NEARI Press

Bergman, J. RDT. Geese Theater Company; East Swanzey, New Hampshire. Personal Communication.

Bergman, J. and Hewish, S. (1996). An introduction to Drama Therapy with Juvenile and Adult Sex Offenders. Brandon, VT: Safer Society Press.

Casey, K. (1996). Masks. Rourke Publications, Inc.

Doyle, Matt (2002) New Hope Treatment Centers. Personal Communication.

Forbess-Greene, S. (1983) The Encyclopedia of Icebreakers: Structured activities that warm-up, motivate, challenge, acquaint and energize. San Diego, CA. Applied Skills Press. ISBN 0-89889-005-0

Gardner, Howard (1983). Frames of mind: The theory of multiple intelligences. New York: Basic Books.

Gates, F. (1979). Easy to make Monster Masks and Disguises. Harvey House Publications

Haaven, Jim (2001) Oregon State Hospital, Salem Oregon Personal Communication.

Longo, R.E. (2001) Paths to wellness: A holistic approach. Holyoke, MA: NEARI Press.

Longo, R.E. (2002) A Integrated Experiential Approach to Treating Young People Who Sexually Abuse, in Geffner, Robert (ed) 2002.Sex Offenders: Assessment and Treatment. Family Violence and Sexual Assault Institute

Lowenstein, L. (1999) Creative Interventions for Troubled Children and Youth. Champion Press Toronto, Ontario Canada.

New Hope treatment Centers (2002). Guidelines for the Use of Touch in Therapy.

Robinson, S. L. (2002) Growing Beyond: A Workbook for Adolescent Girls. Holyoke, MA: NEARI Press.

Steene, C. (1993)The Relapse Prevention Book for Youth. Safer Society Press Brandon, Vermont 1993.

Thompson, James (1999) Drama Workshops for Anger Management and Offending Behavior. London: Jessica Kingsley Publishers.

Tyo, Cindy (2002) New Hope Treatment Centers. Personal Communication.

APPENDIX A

Guidelines for Use of Touch[10]

The following guidelines are designed to help staff and patients work with touch while maintaining healthy and safe boundaries. They are subdivided into key issues regarding the use of touch with patients.

These guidelines are not applicable to the use of restraint with patients. When a patient behaves in a fashion in which he/she poses a threat or harm to him/her self or others, program policy regarding management of aggressive behaviors and use of restraint are to be followed.

I. Touch is not for every patient.

The use of touch and one's individual comfort level with touch are determined by a variety of factors. Age, culture, and family values, and life experiences play a role in one's level of comfort regarding touch.

Given individual differences and other factors it is important that you *know the patient well* before you discuss touch and then engage in the use of touch with a particular patient. You can turn to a variety of materials to assess touch comfort. Previous assessments can help determine a patient's comfort with being touched or potential problems if touch is used. It is important, however, to recognize that previous evaluations may not always be accurate.

Staff observation is one of the best resources to determine a patient's comfort level regarding touch. After a patient is admitted to a program the issue of touch can be discussed with the patient and *self-report* can be used to see if staff observations and previous evaluations are accurate.

When there is uncertainty about the use of touch with a particular patient then *treatment team review* can be utilized to make determinations regarding the use of touch.

Line staff need guidance from therapists regarding not only the use of touch, but how and when touch should be used with particular patients. To best understand these principles it is highly recommended that all staff have some basic training in boundaries and boundary issues before engaging in touch with patients.

One critical piece of information about using touch is making sure patients understand that they *can feel comfortable saying "no" to touch*. Often patients have a hard time saying no to other issues that happen in treatment programs. With touch we want to make sure they understand that it is their bodies and they can say no to anyone, including staff, they do not want touching them. They may *feel peer pressure or staff pressure* as a result of the power differential regarding touch. *Patient education/training about touch/boundaries* should be conducted. Staff must be able to *discuss touch issues with patients*.

Touch is fluid. A staff or patient may feel comfortable with touch one moment and not the next. *Feelings about touch can and will vary*.

[10] Guidelines for use of Touch (2002), New Hope Treatment Centers, Charleston, SC.

II. Touch is contraindicated for some patients.

Our patients come from a variety of backgrounds and experiences. Unfortunately, most of our patients have experienced childhood abuse and neglect and in many cases the abuse was physical and/or sexual. Children who have had *traumatic experiences* may be uncomfortable, afraid of, and even act violently as a result of being touched in any way. Some patients may have *behavioral issues* that warrant we not use touch with them during periods they are in treatment. Some behavioral problems that would preclude the safe use of touch are *boundary problems*, *sexual acting out*, *aggression issues,* and *sexualized behavior* in response to being touched. *Cultural and/or family values* may also be reasons to not engage the use of touch with a particular patient.

When there is a concern about using touch with a particular patient, *treatment team discussion and review during the course of treatment* should be done on a routine basis. Always refer to previous clinical reports, psycho-social assessments, and other documents as a potential resource for this type of information on patients.

III. Touch is not for every staff person.

Staff must also be comfortable with the use of touch. Based on cultural, family and other influences, some staff may not believe in or engage in touch with patients which is perfectly fine and natural. One critical point, however, is that *staff should not differentiate between patients* regarding the use of touch. All patients should be treated equally as touching one patient and not another can indicate favorites and giving certain patients special attention (i.e., as a general rule staff should not hug one patient and deny a hug to the next based upon personal likes or dislikes). Such behavior on the part of staff is often more damaging then helpful.

Not every staff person will be comfortable engaging in touch with patients. We must also *teach staff to feel comfortable saying "no" to touch* and other requests made by patients when they may feel program pressure or other pressures to participate in treatment activities, etc. Touch is a personal choice. Again, there may be family and/or cultural issues that come into play when staff make decisions about the use of touch.

Staff education on touch is necessary. Staff need to understand boundary issues, impact issues related to unwanted touch, and education to address how they can respond in a healthy way when learning about and seeing touch. See Figure 1, Continuum of Touch.

IV. Touch is an individual choice for both parties, (patient and staff/ patient and patient).

When people engage in touch, regardless of type, it should always be a two-way agreement. We have all had the experience of a simple gesture of extending one's hand for a handshake only to be met with a rather meek quick shake or no reciprocation from the other party. As staff, *we can't assume that by simply giving a patient the choice that the patient understands the implications*. We must clarify with the patient that his/her choice is one's own and not the result of power differentials or pressure from others. If a patient does not choose to engage in touch or activities or experiential exercises that involve touch, there should never be any consequences for the patient.

V. Touch involves an understanding and agreement between both parties

Our patients come to NHTC with different needs, and varied disabilities. In some cases age, developmental stage, and learning disabilities can effect whether a patient is confident and comfortable in agreeing to treatment matters and issues. *We cannot assume that a patient can understand and agree to touch. We must clarify with the patient* his/her understanding about touch, touch guidelines, saying no and so forth. We must also remember that touch is fluid and patient or staff person's decision to engage in touch may change from one moment to the next.

VI. Types of touch (peer to peer & staff to patient)

There are various types or levels of touch. The first type of touch is general greetings (formal and informal) that include professional greetings, i.e., hand shakes and friendship greetings, i.e., high 5, dap, etc. General greetings, how they are done, and when they are done can vary among both staff and patients. We need to be sensitive to cultural differences, gender differences, individual differences and individual comfort level, while using both common sense and sound professional judgment. Hugs are not to be considered as a general greeting for all persons.

The next type/level of touch is normalized/socialized touch. This type of touch is normal in most social settings, relationships, and social contacts. This type of touch includes pats on the back, hugs, side hugs, and other forms of healthy social skills that one finds within families, between friends, etc., and sports activities that require physical contact. Touch with patients should always be done in a professional manner taking into account a variety of issues including the patient's age and what would constitute developmentally appropriate touch. This type of touch should always be done in the presence of one or more staff.

Touch used during therapeutic activities, i.e., in treatment groups, in experiential exercises, milieu activities, etc., is the third level or type of touch (i.e., group hug). This type of touch is always done in the presence of clinical staff and by clinical staff. This type of touch is always done with a specific and therapeutic purpose in mind, i.e., it is a part of a group activity, experiential exercise, or role-play. Touch to be used is explained to the patient.

The following serves as a continuum of touch within NHTC facilities.

Figure 1 Continuum of Touch with Patients

No Touch	General Greetings	Normalized Touch	Therapeutic Touch	Inappropriate Touch	Abusive Touch
	handshakes	sports/rec activities	experiential	hand holding	hitting
	high 5	pat on the back	role-plays	extended hugs	slap
	dap	side hug	drama work	any sexual touch	punch
		hug	group hug		sexual-behavior

VII. When touch is appropriate.

Touch is fluid and therefore it is not possible to determine when all types or levels of touch are deemed appropriate. These guidelines help NHTC staff better assess the use and appropriateness of touch.

Peer to peer touch should occur using the following guidelines:

First, there should always be one or more staff persons present, even when using general greeting. This helps avoid false accusations regarding patient-to-patient contact.

Normalized touch should always occur in front of one or more staff persons. This type or level of touch should be reviewed by the Therapist/Case Manager and/or treatment team when necessary. There should always be a therapeutic reason for this type of touch to occur, whether between two patients or patient and staff person.

Touch in therapy should always occur in the presence of one or more clinical staff. This type of touch is activity-based. This type or level of touch should be reviewed by the Therapist/Case Manager and/or treatment team when necessary. There should always be a therapeutic reason for this type of touch to occur, whether between two patients or patient and staff person.

VIII. Always in the presence of another staff person.

With the exception of general greetings, all types of touch should be done in the presence of one or more staff persons. Peer to peer touch should not occur unless there is a staff person present. Staff to patient touch should always occur in the presence of one or more staff persons. Therapeutic touch should always be done in the presence of one or more clinical staff.

IX. Boundaries.

There are several issues that need to be addressed when determining whether to engage in touch with a patient and if a particular patient will benefit from engaging in touch. Personal boundaries is a critical part of using touch.

Each individual has a set of personal boundaries that govern his/her life. NHTC patients are often lacking in healthy boundaries which may result from environmental and familial influences.

When we look at people who are likely to invade personal boundaries of others or display poor boundaries with others, they are people who may suffer from chronic anger problems (and may deliberately exploit others), poor social skills development, or lacking in healthy values and beliefs about how one treats other people.

For example, people who are passive in nature (who do not exercise personal power) often have no boundaries and allow people to use them or take advantage of them. People who are aggressive (who try to control and over power others) overstep the boundaries of others. For example, people who are passive in nature (who do not exercise personal power) often have no boundaries and allow people to use them or take advantage of them. People who are aggressive (who try to control and over power others) overstep the boundaries of others.

People who are appropriately assertive (who see themselves and others equally and are just concerned about power over themselves and exercise self-control) know how to appropriately set boundaries. People who are appropriately assertive (who see themselves and others equally and are just concerned about power over themselves and exercise self-control) know how to appropriately set boundaries.

Boundary styles are often described as a) non-existent, b) walled, and c) healthy. For people who are passive, they usually do not recognize boundaries for themselves or for others. People who are angry and aggressive are often walled. They do not let others in and are protective of the self. People with healthy boundaries respect themselves and respect others. They get their needs met through appropriate assertiveness and self-expression, and do not use, exploit, or take advantage of others.

When we consider the use of touch in programming, we must take into account boundaries for one's self as well as boundaries we observe in others. People's boundaries are different based upon their culture, upbringing, and personal values and beliefs systems. Individual boundaries must be respected while at the same time addressed when they work in a clinical setting.

In some cases, one's boundaries may need to be worked with when they fall outside of the boundaries a program sets regarding work with the patients. If personal boundaries are too loose, there is a potential for problems to arise within a clinical setting. If one's boundaries are too rigid, the efficacy of treatment may be impacted. At the very least we must recognize others' boundaries, their differences, and be respectful toward them.

One important issue related to boundaries is the relationship between patient and staff. It is difficult sometimes to keep boundaries when working with children; the temptation is to parent them. Staff must be vigilant about keeping the relationship as a friendly professional one and not one of professional friendship.

Transference and counter transference are other areas in which staff must be trained and educated. Understanding these important therapeutic elements will help staff keep professional boundaries.

When touch is used, staff should take time to talk with patients about touch, the types of touch, the use of touch in programming, and teach them appropriate ways of both expressing their feelings regarding touch as well as what types of touch are appropriate between patients and between staff and patients.

Patients should be oriented to all program rules and policies including the use of touch. Each patient should be assessed to determine if the patient is okay with touch or whether there are clinical and or personal reasons why a particular patient should not engage in touch between staff and patient or patient to patient. Reasons may include but are not limited to: 1) previous trauma/abuse, 2) aggression problems; and 3) the patient has a history of engaging in sexual touch with other patients and/or staff.

X. Developmental issues and touch.

Levels one and two touch (general greetings and normal/socialized touch) are important clinical aspects regarding children with attachment disorders. An increasing amount of literature is now speaking to the value of using touch in facilitating attachment.

As children grow older and enter the teen years, their need/desire for touch can become more fluid. Some will want hugs while others may not. Age issues need to be addressed when engaging patients in touch.

Gender differences must also be addressed in regard to the use of touch. Differences between male and female patients and how they view and/or use touch must be noted and respected. Issues related to touch by male staff and female patients and female staff and male patients may also be apparent. Patients with gender identity problems may be more sensitive to touch by same sex staff or patients. A patient who is homophobic may perceive touch by a same sexed person as threatening. Patients who are exploring homosexual (gay/lesbian) lifestyles may perceive touch by a same sexed person as a come on or sexual, regardless of the nature of the touch.

Some patients may have identified problems regarding their beliefs about touch. Some may see touch solely as a way of being sexual. Others may be retraumatized (i.e., a female patient who was sexually abused by an adult male). Others may have no problems being touched by women, but may experience traumatic feelings if touched by a male staff person.

The patient's level of functioning can also play a role in how they perceive touch. Normal functioning patients may experience a variety of problems regarding touch between patients or between staff and patients. Lower functioning patients may experience more problems with touch. Lower functioning clients are more likely to experience touch differently than it was intended, i.e., interpreting a hug as a sexual come-on, interpreting any level or type of touch as sexual when in fact it is not.

XI. General education on touch for staff.

When programs develop guidelines and/or policies regarding the use of touch in clinical settings, staff education is important. As noted above the use of touch is a complex issue and there are many related areas that must be addressed. In order to assure the appropriate use of touch within programs, NHTC will provide training in the following areas:

• Child development
• Attachment theory
• Values clarification
• Professional boundaries and the therapeutic relationship
• Use of touch in clinical programming

XII General education on touch for patients.

In addition to staff, patients need similar education on touch and education on related subjects such as values clarification, boundaries, and healthy non-sexual relationships. Education on touch should be done in both a group format with follow-up and in an individual counseling session.

XIII. Alternatives to touch.

When touch is contraindicated for certain patients or when staff persons do not feel comfortable engaging in any level of touch, there are limited alternatives for certain types of touch.

For level one - generalized greetings, a simple wave or thumbs up gesture can signal a "hello" or greeting. Patients can make up verbal greeting "flash cards" that say hello, good morning, etc. and use those in lieu of a handshake or high five.

For level two - normalized/socialized touch there are few substitutes.

For level three - touch in therapy, there are some substitutes for experiential exercises that may work. For example, instead of holding hands, patients may both take the end of a bandana that signifies holding hands.

Generally speaking, however, there are few substitutes for touch. When one has restriction or concerns regarding touch they must be honored. Creative ways of working in group, congratulating others, and greeting others that show warmth, caring, and concern, should be explored and used whenever possible.

XIV. Cultural issues.

As noted above, NHTC patients and staff both come from a variety of cultures and regions throughout the United States, and in some cases abroad. Each of us, both patients and staff comes to NHTC with our own set of values and beliefs that reflect our families, cultures and diverse backgrounds.

As staff it is our job to help educate others and teach respect and tolerance to those whose values and beliefs differ from ours. We must be willing to accept cultural and family differences in values and not push patients or staff to engage in touch when they are not comfortable doing so.

When we find patients with unhealthy boundaries and/or with problems related to touch, we must always think of what is best for that person therapeutically. We do not want to push our values and beliefs on others. We must uphold program policy, procedure, rules and regulations without infringing on the beliefs of others in ways that are not therapeutic.

APPENDIX B

Overview of the History, Use, and Basic Mask Construction

Historical Use of Masks

The following is a brief outline of masks and mask construction (Case, 1996; Gates, 1979).

A. Historically masks were made out of:
Animal hides/fur
Stone
Metal
Wood
Shells
Cloth
Corn husks
Straw

There are a variety of masks that have been used for many reasons in cultures all over the world. Historically we find masks were used constructed and used for:

Hunting - Masks were made to represent animals. A ritual called pantomime magic resulted in the construction of masks designed to make hunts successful. If a man pretended to shoot another man with an animal head, he would be able to do likewise in the real hunt.

Power – Masks gave people power. Using masks would give the man the power of the animal and/or could change people into powerful warriors and fearsome beasts.

Cover the dead – Masks were designed to help the spirit find the dead body when it was time to return to the body. These were made of stone, gold, turquoise.

Plays - Masks were used to show whether their characters were happy or sad, or to distinguish between characters identities.

Religion - Native Americans along the pacific Coats used masks to celebrate their heritage and religion. Most were made of wood . Some were used to tell stories about the past.

Honor spirits of people - Some African tribes believe that the spirits of dead people stay with their tribe, so the mask is used to remember each person and to let the spirit know that it is still important to the tribe.

Rites of passage - Some tribes in Central Africa use masks to celebrate the change from boyhood to manhood. The young boy wears a mask that represents his childhood, and then he throws away the mask to signify the end of child-hood.
Healing – The Shaman or wise person in Eskimo tribes use masks while dancing and chanting a secret chant to make the spirits happy again.

Celebration - Mexican celebrations use masks. Mayordomo is the person in the village who is in charge of the masks and must select and train those who will dance with the masks.

Concealing identity - Soldiers and warriors used masks to make it hard for others to see them. The camouflage paint on US soldier outfits is an example of a mask.

The mask was soon incorporated into the arts. We see the use of masks in the following:

Performing art
Music
Dance
Drama
Visual art
Sculpture
Painting
Writing
Creating dialogue, scripts

Masks are also used in assisting children to understand literature. They might be used in the following ways:

For younger children, masks are used to act out stories as they are read out loud. Teachers or parents might assign children different characters and have them create masks and costumes for that character. Once constructed the children perform the story using the masks and costumes.

For older children it is fun to read them a story and then have them change the perspective of the story by produce a new script. After producing a new script, teachers and caregivers might assign children the new different characters and have them create masks and costumes for that character. Once constructed the children perform the revised story with the new perspective using the masks and costumes.

Making Plaster Craft Masks

There are several ways to construct a basic mask. One method is to find a hard plastic mask or the head of a mannequin to use as a mold. Take liquid latex and cover the plastic mask or mannequin head with several layers of latex letting each layer dry before applying the next layer. Peel the newly created latex mask off and paint it with a particular expression.

Using Plaster Craft Strips for Mask Construction

Plaster craft strips can be purchased at most arts and crafts supply centers. Make a mask by:

1. Make a newspaper mold or form of a head.
2. Cut plaster craft into strips.
3. Dip one strip into water and place on mold.

Hint: every time you lay a strip down, smooth it with your fingers for a smooth finish overall.
4. Repeat step 3 until form is covered. Strips should go in one direction - horizontal.
5. On next layer, repeat steps 3 & 4 laying the strips across the last \layer - change direction   to vertical.
6. Lay down one more layer and change direction - this time to diagonal.

Allow masks to dry at least overnight, maybe longer. Decorate with paint yarn, glitter, sequins, or anything that comes to mind.

o paint masks:

Mix Tempera paints 2:1 with white glue (Elmer's). Paint the mask with sturdy brushes. Rinse brushes immediately and thoroughly in warm soapy water to avoid ruining brushes with glue. Acrylic paint will also work but is much more expensive then the Tempera glue mixture.

APPENDIX C

FLASH CARD STATEMENTS

I feel . . .

Sometimes I feel . . .

I don't like to feel because . . .

I'm not supposed to feel because . . .

I remember feeling . . .

I'm afraid of . . .

I remember . . .

I remember thinking . . .

Sometimes I think . . .

I like to forget because . . .

I tell myself . . .

It is all my fault that . . .

It is my fault that . . .

I will . . .

I want . . .

I need . . .

I want to do . . .

I want to hurt you because . . .

I hate you . . .

I wish You . . .

I'll show _____

Rules . . .

Following rules . . .

School . . .

I'm tired of being told . . .

Everybody tells me . . .

Hell is for children . . .

Holidays . . .

Christmas . . .

My birthday . . .

Everybody . . .

Nobody . . .

No one . . .

My friends . . .

My best friend . . .

At night . . .

My dreams . . .

I trust . . .

I don't trust . . .

You don't even bother to . . .

If you really cared you would . . .

You don't love me . . .

I really do love you . . .

You never loved me . . .

I am . . .

I am a total . . .

My Dad . . .

My childhood . . .

My Mom . . .

My sister . . .

My brother . . .

My family . . .

God . . .

If only . . .

I never . . .

I always . . .

I should have . . .

My life is . . .

Life . . .

Why bother . . .

Why . . .

The truth . . .

I lie . . .

Drugs . . .

I get high to . . .

If I had one wish it would be . . .

I used to . . .

I never should have . . .

I'm not afraid . . .

I deserve . . .

I am . . .

You are . . .

They are . . .

Please . . .

Don't . . .

One day . . .

APPENDIX D

SUPPLEMENTS FOR EXERCISES

EXERCISE I - 4 · TIME CAPSULE - TIME CAPSULE WORKSHEET:

On _____ you will be joining us for the following session. As part of the session you will be engaged in an activity that involves sharing personal memorabilia that gives others an encapsulated view of your life. Please bring six pieces of memorabilia (articles that describe your life such as pictures, plaques, written articles, clothing, books, etc.) to the session. We will share these articles, hence pieces of our lives, with others at the session. You will take the items with you after the session.

EXERCISE M-1 · MY PAPER DOLL

SEVEN POWER CENTERS OR CHAKRAS

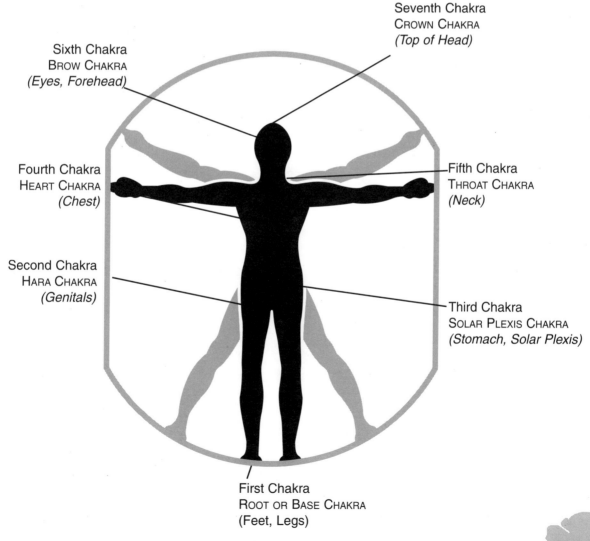

Seventh Chakra
CROWN CHAKRA
(Top of Head)

Sixth Chakra
BROW CHAKRA
(Eyes, Forehead)

Fourth Chakra
HEART CHAKRA
(Chest)

Fifth Chakra
THROAT CHAKRA
(Neck)

Second Chakra
HARA CHAKRA
(Genitals)

Third Chakra
SOLAR PLEXIS CHAKRA
(Stomach, Solar Plexis)

First Chakra
ROOT OR BASE CHAKRA
(Feet, Legs)

APPENDIX E

MASK RESOURCES

There are several places one can acquire masks. Costume stores and theatre stores are two resources.

Masks for use in the exercises in this book contact the Trestle Theatre Company for a brochure:

The Trestle Theatre Company
Birch Centre, Hill End Lane
St. Albans, Hertfordshire
England, AL4 0RA

Phone: 01-7-278-50989
Fax: 01-7 278-55558

E-mail: admin@trestle.org.uk

NEARI PRESS TITLES

Moving Beyond by Thomas F. Leversee, LCSW (2002). NEARI Press, 70 North Summer Street, Holyoke, MA 01040. Paperback, 88 pages. $20.00 plus shipping and handling. Bulk discounts available. **ISBN# 1-929657-16-1**

Moving Beyond Student Manual by Thomas F. Leversee, LCSW (2002). NEARI Press, 70 North Summer Street, Holyoke, MA 01040. Paperback, 52 pages. $10.00 plus shipping and handling. Bulk discounts available. **ISBN# 1-929657-18-8**

Growing Beyond by Susan L. Robinson (2002). NEARI Press, 70 North Summer Street, Holyoke, MA 01040. Paperback, approx. 214 pages. $20.00 plus shipping and handling. **ISBN# 1-929657-17-X**

Growing Beyond Treatment Manual by Susan L. Robinson (2002). NEARI Press, 70 North Summer Street, Holyoke, MA 01040. Paperback, approx. 40 pages. $15.00 plus shipping and handling. **ISBN# 1-929657-15-3**

The Safe Workbook for Youth by John McCarthy and Kathy MacDonald (2001). NEARI Press, 70 North Summer Street, Holyoke, MA 01040. Paperback, 210 pages $20.00 plus shipping and handling. **ISBN# 1-929657-14-5**

Paths To Wellness by Robert E. Longo (2001). NEARI Press, 70 North Summer Street, Holyoke, MA 01040. Paperback, 144 pages. $20.00 plus shipping and handling. Bulk discounts available. **ISBN#1-929657-19-6**

New Hope For Youth: Experiential Exercises for Children & Adolescents by Robert E. Longo and Deborah P. Longo (2003). NEARI Press, 70 North Summer Street, Holyoke, MA 01040. Paperback,150 pages. $35.00 plus shipping and handling. **ISBN# 1-929657-20-X**

Men & Anger: Understanding and Managing Your Anger by Murray Cullen and Robert E. Longo (1999). NEARI Press, 70 North Summer Street, Holyoke, MA 01040. Paperback, 125 pages. $15.00 plus shipping and handling. Bulk discounts available. **ISBN#1-929657-12-9**

Who Am I and Why Am I In Treatment by Robert E. Longo with Laren Bays (2000). NEARI Press, 70 North Summer Street, Holyoke, MA 01040. Paperback, 85 pages. $12.00 plus shipping and handling. Bulk discounts available. **ISBN#1-929657-01-3**

Why Did I Do It Again & How Can I Stop? by Robert E. Longo with Laren Bays (1999). NEARI Press, 70 North Summer Street, Holyoke, MA 01040. Paperback, 192 pages.$20.00 plus shipping and handling. Bulk discounts available. **ISBN#1-929657-11-0**

Enhancing Empathy by Robert E. Longo and Laren Bays (1999). NEARI Press, 70 North Summer Street, Holyoke, MA 01040. Paperback, 77 pages. $12.00 plus shipping and handling. Bulk discounts available. **ISBN#1-929657-04-8**

Standards of Care for Youth in Sex Offense Specific Residential Treatment by S. Bengis, A. Brown, R. Longo, B. Matsuda, K. Singer, and J. Thomas (1997, 1998, 1999). NEARI Press, 70 North Summer Street, Holyoke, MA 01040. $40.00 plus shipping and handling. Bulk discounts available. **ISBN# 1-929657-05-6**

Shipping

$4.50 for first copy / .50¢ ea. additional copy

Order from:

NEARI Press
70 North Summer Street
Holyoke, MA 01040
413.540.0712

Whitman Communications, Inc.
PO Box 1220/10 Water Street
Lebanon, NH 03766-4220
1-800-353-3730